FROM
RICHARD KIMBLE
TO
BARACK OBAMA

AMERICA AS VIEWED BY
AN EGYPTIAN-AMERICAN
WHO LOVES HER

HOSSAM NASSER

BALBOA.
PRESS
A DIVISION OF HAY HOUSE

ISBN: 978-1-4525-6122-6 (sc)
ISBN: 978-1-4525-6123-3 (e)

Library of Congress Control Number: 2012919370
Balboa Press books may be ordered through booksellers or by contacting:

Balboa Press
A Division of Hay House
1663 Liberty Drive
Bloomington, IN 47403
www.balboapress.com
1-(877) 407-4847

Because of the dynamic nature of the Internet, any web addresses or links contained in this book may have changed since publication and may no longer be valid. The views expressed in this work are solely those of the author and do not necessarily reflect the views of the publisher, and the publisher hereby disclaims any responsibility for them.

The author of this book does not dispense medical advice or prescribe the use of any technique as a form of treatment for physical, emotional, or medical problems without the advice of a physician, either directly or indirectly. The intent of the author is only to offer information of a general nature to help you in your quest for emotional and spiritual well-being. In the event you use any of the information in this book for yourself, which is your constitutional right, the author and the publisher assume no responsibility for your actions.

Any people depicted in stock imagery provided by Thinkstock are models, and such images are being used for illustrative purposes only. Certain stock imagery © Thinkstock.

Printed in the United States of America

Balboa Press rev. date: 11/13/2012

Table of Contents

Preface

In a troubled world filled with conflicts and mistrust, it becomes imperative that we develop a proper understanding of other people who share the planet with us. How they think, why they act the way they do, and why does everybody hate America, or do they?

As someone who has one foot planted in the land of the Pharaohs, and the other deeply rooted into the land of opportunity, I am going to tell you my story, or better yet, my side of the story. I will share with you the perspective of a man born and raised in the Middle East, but chose for his home America, and I will let you in on what goes on in the minds and hearts of people in this vital and troubled part of the world.

I will take you through a long journey that starts way back in the sixties with the then very popular TV show "The Fugitive" and ends with a man who recently made the powerful claim that "Yes We Can." I will give you the unique perspective of someone who understands both sides of the Atlantic, and will let you in on a different view for events for which local views have long been packaged and shelved for so many years. Take a look from another angle; you are bound to see something else! In the process of reading this book, you may even gain insights that may help you see the world in a different light.

"From Richard Kimble to Barack Obama" is a mixture of personal experiences intertwined with political events that span over five decades. You will read a totally fresh perspective about political events along with a completely different assessment of those major players who helped shape them. After reading this book, you will realize how the so called "conventional wisdom" may, after all, be just a synonym to mental complacency. You will end up with a new understanding of issues such as the infamous Palestinian-Israeli conflict, Iraq, Iran, and Afghanistan among others. In each case, an historic synopsis is presented. This, at times, may relate to relatively recent history while at others it may be quite distant.

The main underlying motive for writing *"From Richard Kimble to Barack Obama"* is my very deep love for this country. It is as simple as that. I offer you my own distilled life experience on a silver platter in the hope that it may help us all make better decisions when it comes to dealing with the rest of the world.

"From Richard Kimble to Barack Obama" is a political memoir based on the views and life experiences of its writer, and although others may have written along similar lines, one distinction needs to be noted, which is the fact that this is the one book that approaches

the subject matter through a mindset of eastern and western cultures, simultaneously. Having been born and raised in a Middle Eastern country, and living the rest of my life in the United States, I will present you with a unique perspective of world events and how they may be interpreted in a surprisingly different way.

Utmost respect is due to writers such as Jimmy Carter for his books such as: *"We Can Have Peace in the Holy Land; A Plan That Will Work,"* and *"Palestine Peace Not Apartheid,"* and Zbigniew Brzezinski for his writings such as: *"America and the World: Conversations on the Future of American Foreign Policy,"* and *"Second Chance: Three Presidents and the Crisis of American Superpower."* Whereas these are superb writings that treat world politics with an extraordinary understanding, they, nonetheless, are the product of purely western minds and are, hence, void of that view of the other. This is the main gap that *"From Richard Kimble to Barack Obama"* will attempt to fill.

"From Richard Kimble to Barack Obama" is written for everyone who seeks a better understanding of the complex world we live in. Detailed analyses are provided to explain volatile political conflicts that we find ourselves sucked into and having to find a way to safely extricate ourselves from. The book even presents formulas for how to deal in each and every one of these problem areas be it the Palestinian-Israeli conflict, the two active wars in Iraq and Afghanistan, or the escalating tension in relations with Iran. This book is written for every American who cares enough about this great nation to make a serious effort at learning about the other side of the story, and in doing so may discover an uncharted path to world peace.

Acknowledgments

No work is ever the product of one person's efforts, and *"From Richard Kimble to Barack Obama"* is by no means an exception to the rule. I, hereby, would like to extend my deepest thanks to Grete Stenersen, my colleague at Saint Mary's College for her insightful feedback at the very early stages of this work. Grete was the first person to read through the initial manuscript and her encouraging remarks gave me the push I needed to go on with my project.

Thanks are also due to my very good friend and my one and only editor, John Paulin for his efforts which I know for a fact have greatly improved the quality of the finished version of the book.

Many thanks are due to Virginia Morrel and Adriane Pontecorvo of the Balboa Press publishing team who had always exhibited both friendly and professional collaboration throughout the production phases of this work.

Thanks are also due to the folks of Wikipedia for facilitating my historic searches which exponentially facilitated my effort in that regard. Although some historic references were obtained from other sources, most of which were based on information found in Wikipedia.

And last, but not least, my thanks and gratitude to my beloved wife Dodie who despite not being in the best shape at the time of this writing had undertaken the responsibility of preparing the marketing plan for my book. She is also credited for first convincing her stubborn husband to include photos in the book, and then going through the search and collection of those photos; some of which — as you will find out — are public record whereas others are from our personal library.

The Early Years

So there I was, a ten year old boy sitting in the living room that Friday night in 1964 anxious to watch a show that captivated the imagination of millions of viewers all over the country for months on end. That country was Egypt and the living room was in Alexandria.

ABC's *The Fugitive* mesmerized me, and I was hooked for life on American showbiz. The protagonist, Dr. Richard Kimble, had been wrongly convicted of murdering his wife and sentenced to death. And upon escaping from the derailed train that was delivering him to death row, he vowed to find his wife's real killer—the infamous one armed man.

What was captivating about the series was the fact that Dr. Kimble—portrayed brilliantly by David Janssen—was determined to fight the entire system in order to prove his innocence. That individualistic approach to life was fascinating for a ten year old boy conservatively brought up in the upper middle class Egyptian family of a well-respected college professor. And even though I completely identified with Richard Kimble and his fight for justice, I still felt the utmost respect for Philip Gerard, the relentless police lieutenant from the fictional town of Stafford, Indiana. Detective Gerard was a man trying to do his job to the best of his abilities. This was yet another trait that added to my fascination of this distant land called "America," and I quickly developed a sense of admiration for these traits that so distinctly identified those folks across the Atlantic.

2

The Fugitive aired on a weekly basis, and ran for a number of years, by which time I was completely sold on the American brand. Was that because I was an idealistic kid who wanted to believe that there was a place out there where somebody could fight the system from the outside and yet be exonerated if his case were proven? Or was it because everyone was striving to do their best, which drove the entire system forward and caused it to flourish? Whatever it was, it seemed to be working, even though mistakes were possible and, in fact, inevitable. And although there were no guarantees in life, this whole bonanza of a social experiment seemed to tick along just fine.

In those days, I loved hearing my Dad's stories about his time studying *agricultural sciences at the University of Missouri* in the good old USA during the late forties and early fifties. He lived in Kansas City, Missouri, and I loved looking at photos of him all bundled up, standing knee deep in the winter snow. He even kept the set of AAA maps with his driving route to the East Coast marked off in black ink when he headed back home. This exhibition was usually associated with a few personal anecdotes about his life in the US. The story that still sticks in my mind was about how he used to sign his checks at his favorite diner in pencil! And I would gasp upon hearing that and start asking him "what if…," but he would always assure me that people were honest and life was good. I must admit, however, that this was one practice I never took up into my own life. Nonetheless, it was yet another indicator as to how safe life can be among people who are fundamentally good and genuinely friendly.

During those years, my favorite cousin Dalal was living in Washington D.C. while her husband was assigned on some diplomatic mission at the embassy. During her summer visits, she would usually bring back gifts for us youngsters. These were mostly clothing items of the finest quality, and I showed mine off proudly. I developed a sense that there was something credible about a product that carried the claim, "Made in the USA."

• •

There was one item in particular that she brought to my father–her uncle–which was especially impressive, and that was a huge luxurious green barbeque grill, the center piece of many a backyard cookout in beautiful Alexandria during the warm summer nights when the Mediterranean breeze filled the atmosphere with its special and unforgettable aroma. After each use of the Cadillac BBQ, Dad would personally clean it to the point that it sparkled as if it were back on display in the showroom. He would not allow anyone less qualified than himself to interfere, nor would he allow his pride and joy to remain at the mercy of the elements. The green beauty always returned to its special place under the stairs where it rested 'til its next call to duty. This family member held its rightful place in our household for at least fifteen years, retiring only during its last few years after Dad had passed away. Somehow, many of the fun activities died with him. Dad, may you rest in peace. I know you would have had a lot to do with me and my own family if you stayed around longer. Moved by your stories, I have retraced the journey you made to America six decades ago, and I am still here. I just chose a place with a better climate!

• •

In the summer of 1952 the military overthrew King Farouk and replaced the monarchy with a republic. Gamal Abdel Nasser, a youthful and charismatic military man, was its president. In May of 1967, poorly advised by his confidant and right arm, the top military man, Abdel Hakim Amer, about the state of readiness of the military to go into battle, Nasser decided to blockade the straits of Tiran. This narrow passage between the southern tip of the Sinai Peninsula and northwest Saudi Arabia at the southern end of Gulf of Aquaba is Israel's only outlet to the Red Sea and the Indian Ocean. Israeli ships now had no direct access to eastern Africa or Asia, so this act was tantamount to a declaration of war and was one of the crucial events leading to the six-day-war in June of that year.

The war resulted in a resounding defeat of the Arab forces, and landed the most severe blow to Nasser's status within Egypt and the Arab World as a whole. More importantly, it broke his spirit, and he was never the same after that. It was later ascertained that Nasser had in fact died in 1967, although he was not buried until 1970.

On a personal note, the war coincided with the final exams of our middle school, the EBS (English Boys School), and these were the national exams required for enrollment in high school. We had already sat for the first three days of the exams, and two more were left when the war broke, so our exams were halted. This hiatus continued for a good three or four weeks before testing was resumed, and as might be expected the disruption adversely affected many students. However, the consequences were most deeply felt at the national level in the humiliation that every Egyptian felt during the following six years.

During my years at the EBS, I had befriended one of the three Jewish brothers who were my schoolmates there. Zaki Shashoua was a mild-mannered, kind-hearted young man who enjoyed a good game of soccer during recess as much as did I. We had nothing but good feelings towards one another, and our friendship transcended our religious or political differences. However, as a consequence of the 1967 War, his family decided that it was in its best interest to immigrate to Israel. I have not heard from him since—I missed him then, and I hope we meet again someday.

6

Hossam and Nelly

(Private collection)

The Nasser family

(Private collection)

Mom and my sister Nelly with the famous BBQ

(Private collection)

Free officers Council

http://en.wikipedia.org/wiki/Egyptian_
Revolutionary_Command_Council

King Farouk of Egypt

He was born on Feb. 11, 1920, in Cairo, Egypt and died on March 18, 1965, in Rome, Italy. He was the king of Egypt from 1936 to 1952. Although initially quite popular, the internal rivalries of his administration and his alienation of the military coupled with his increasing excesses and eccentricities led to his downfall and to the formation of a republic.

http://www.flickr.com/photos/

The Seventies

In the early 70s Richard Nixon made an unprecedented visit to Egypt, and he sure did impress the Egyptian public, most notably because of his decision to travel by train–not the best accommodations—a decision that allowed him to stay close to the masses throughout the trip.

The Egyptian people saw a man who was well informed, articulate, and quite personable, who represented America, and was loved by ordinary people. Thus many Egyptians were not able to understand America's reaction to Watergate. Here was a president who had accomplished a major breakthrough with China, and was farsighted enough to acknowledge its strategic importance at least a good thirty years before that notion became conventional wisdom, and was admired internationally. Yet he was ungracefully dragged down by his own people for a single political misstep. Why couldn't they have allowed him to atone for this transgression instead of throwing the baby out with the wash water? Don't political figures make mistakes? Oh boy, do they ever! Can anyone envision what would have happened had Nixon been allowed to finish his term, what global impact might he have had?

Well, I guess we'll never know because American politics is fast to the trigger. Yet whatever Nixon did during the Watergate scandal would be classified as child's play in the book of many world leaders. Am I advocating lack of accountability of elected officials? Of course not. All I am saying is get real! We cannot expect presidents or anyone else to be perfect, and we will have more to say about this later in the book. Not all human shortcomings deserve such extreme retribution, especially when, otherwise, they're doing a darned good job.

I realize that this is not a popular view among some Americans; especially those who had their hearts bent on bringing this good man down no matter what. However, you have to understand that my perspective is that of someone from the Middle East, where people are deeply touched by any act of kindness. Humane connections like those forged by Nixon in Egypt mean a great deal to people from this part of the world, and Middle Easterners will go out of their way to support those who have treated them with dignity and respect. They are fully aware that in the present historical era, they have taken a back seat in the journey of human accomplishment, but they are also fully aware of, and yes, very proud of the crucial contributions their ancestors made to civilization long before similar advances in social organization and technology had reached most other parts of the world.

Failure to take these basic observations into account may create misunderstandings when dealing with people from the Middle East. Recent events show how things can and do go horribly wrong. If you want a simple formula for how *not* to deal with the Arab World, please refer to American foreign policy during the presidency of George W. Bush. After the World Trade Center was attacked on September 11, 2001, nearly all nations of the world, Muslim and otherwise, were ready and eager to support America and her legitimate pursuit of justice and security. Nevertheless, the Bush administration squandered this massive political capital and nearly universal international support by acting as a bully, despite the fact that this approach has proven its futility time and time again.

13

• •

Mom loved that car. It was a 1952 Oldsmobile Delta 88 that Dad brought home from his American trip. He had driven it from Kansas City to Idlewild (now JFK) Airport in New York with the assistance of those AAA maps he kept as souvenirs. It had a dark green top, a light green bottom, and was indeed a beauty. I still recall how Mom would brag that the ride was so smooth that, when Dad was driving, she could sip coffee without spilling a drop. I guess that was her way of vouching for the car's impeccable suspension. This car was my family's only vehicle for the first twenty years of my life, and Mom stood tearfully on the balcony as it was driven away when Dad finally sold it. From Dad's perspective, the car had more than served its purpose, plus it was a V8 and we were in the mid-seventies when gasoline was much more expensive. Consequently, we switched to the more fuel efficient, newer model Renault. Needless to say, Mom never warmed up to the European new comer. As a matter of fact, the Renault was one item that she quickly disposed of after Dad's departure.

On Politicians and Politics:

14

During the early 70s, Anwar Sadat was having a hard time solidifying his role as Nasser's successor. Many political figures believed that he would never get a firm grip on the presidency, and indeed this task would have been difficult for any Egyptian politician at that time. Some cabinet members even sought to maneuver him out of office by forming a political coalition for that purpose. However, they severely underestimated this savvy politician and lived to regret the attempt. Not only were they outmaneuvered, but they gave Sadat an opportunity to emerge as a stronger leader unchallenged within his party and loved by his people.

He used his sharp and meticulous political vision to plan the 1973 war against Israel, and following the success of his quick military strike, he managed to negotiate the return of all Egyptian land lost in 1967. Not only did he regain the entire Sinai desert, he also topped that achievement with his trip to Tel Aviv, which raised many an eye brow in the region. This trip paved the way to the signing of a peace treaty between the two nations, a treaty that was made possible through the miraculous efforts of President Carter, and this treaty remains in effect to this day.

Jimmy Carter was perceived in the Arab World as a reputable and honest Christian man who could be trusted. Unlike some other American presidents, he had a good grasp of the nuances of the Middle East and its problems. He was, therefore, a much respected figure in this part of the world. Yet at home he did not fare that well. Why was that? Historians cite a lack of leadership and a bad economy. But in the eyes of others he had plenty of character. As for the economy, I keep hearing that this is a factor that presidents may unjustifiably be either credited or blamed for. Indeed, the economy can make or break a president. One former president proclaimed "it's the economy, stupid," but a president may or may not have the power to bring about positive changes. I believe it was Herodotus who said that circumstances rule men, not men the circumstances. This is indeed a dilemma for anyone who needs to maintain an illusion of control.

15

Yet, the factor that contributed most significantly to the plummet of Carter's approval ratings was the Iranian hostage Crisis following the takeover of the American embassy in Tehran in November of 1979 one year before the end of his first and only term. I was then beginning my graduate work at the University of Notre Dame, and I very much admired this man's gallant efforts to free the 52 Americans held hostage by the Iranians while maintaining control of a very bad situation. He did everything humanly possible to bring the hostages home safely and even decided to undertake a daring rescue mission when he realized that the Iranians were not negotiating in good faith. Unfortunately, two of the rescue helicopters crashed during the event killing the Marines on board, exposing the secret mission to whole world, and shutting off any hope he might have had in resolving the crisis through diplomacy.

This was beyond the control of all parties involved including the president, but what can you do when you're dealt bad cards at Poker? I guess you just follow the advice of the old gambler in the Kenny Rogers song and "know when to fold 'em." Well, at that point Carter had no chance at reelection in the face of everything that went so horribly wrong, or against the effervescent Hollywood image of Ronald Reagan. He lost handily.

Now, I would like to talk about how this president fared in his subsequent years. I think it is fair to say that he has redeemed himself through his continuous efforts in world diplomacy and his work with Habitat for Humanity here at home. He had also written a number of highly instructive and insightful books that are a must read. He even earned himself a Nobel Prize for his reconciliation of Egypt and Israel. What more can you expect from this guy? Well into his 80's and still going strong. What a man. If only the American people would show this fine man appreciation for his efforts before doing so in an obituary.

At the time of the 1979 Islamic Revolution led by the Ayatollah Khomeini in Iran, I was in my second or third semester of graduate studies at Notre Dame. At a gathering of a few students from the Middle East studying there at the time to discuss what was happening in Iran, I was amazed and puzzled by many of my colleague's euphoria over this "resurgence" of Islamic rule. They even went as far as to hope for similar occurrences throughout the Muslim world. I was probably the only one at that meeting to recognize and declare that such events had nothing to do with religion and everything to do with politics.

With regard to the Islamic resurgence in Iran, let me make a quick related comment about Sadat. The one serious domestic misstep that may be attributed to Sadat was his attempt to neutralize the communist influence inside the universities by reinforcing the presence of the so-called Islamic Groups. This was based on the overly simplistic notion that communism was anti-religion and that the best way to counter it would be the support of religious entities. This decision ended up costing him his life during a military parade on October 6th 1981 at the hands of these same people he supported to counter the communists.

I was wrapping up my work at Notre Dame when Sadat was assassinated and was awakened the morning following that event by a phone call from my very close friend and exceptional colleague, Joe Cooler. He called to console me over the loss. Later that day, I was visited by camera crews from local South Bend television stations representing the three major networks. They had come for the views of an Egyptian citizen regarding what had just taken place. When asked why the assassination occurred, I responded with the observation that this is the fate of many progressives and visionaries who are too far ahead of their time. Because he made peace with Israel, Sadat was boycotted by the Arab League, and

17

was considered a traitor by fringe groups within his own people. Members of one of these organizations decided that the best solution was to riddle him with bullets. What a shame. What a loss.

Grad School:

An account of my time at Notre Dame should begin with an encounter I had when I was first flying there in August of 1979. My wife and I were on a short connecting flight to South Bend from Chicago's O'Hare Airport, where we had disembarked from our journey across the Atlantic. South Bend is no more than a hundred miles east of Chicago, a mere 25 minutes by plane just enough for takeoff and landing, I guess. Well, it happened that we were seated next to a very compassionate South Bend native. The excitement of a young foreign student at the beginning of a new life must have been quite apparent to him. I remember to this day the exceptionally kind words of this man as he attempted to land me softly onto the hard ground of reality. He told me that for every person I was pleased to leave behind in Egypt, I would most likely encounter his or her counterpart over here. This observation was an eye opener. It put into focus the simple fact that I had overlooked in all my excitement, which is that people are people, they are the same everywhere, and the human condition is what it is. So thank you Fred Bachert for your wisdom and kindness. Although our paths crossed for no more than 25 minutes, and thirty years have elapsed since that fight from Chicago to South Bend, I still remember your name and your advice.

18

We were finally checked into the Morris Inn on campus for our first night in the United States. We did, however, make one last pit stop at Denny's for our first American meal. Our cab driver was kind enough to wait for us while we had our meal and then drive us back. As soon as we got into our room at the Morris Inn, Dodie collapsed in bed, but I was not ready to call it a night. I turned on the TV and watched a man telling jokes to an audience that was quite receptive to his routine, although I found their laughter incomprehensible. Nevertheless, I continued to watch it before finally retiring. Nevertheless, it was to become one of my favorite shows and its host my favorite TV talk show host of all time, Johnny Carson. No day was complete without Johnny and the Tonight Show after that, and it did not take long before I joined the studio audience in laughing at his jokes and the hilarious characters he used to display in his infamous sketches.

Notre Dame had a program in place to assist international students. We were assigned to a host family, which was to ease us into American life by showing us the ropes: where to go grocery shopping, how to find a convenient residence, how to open a bank account and establish credit, and many other similar activities. After this initial orientation, our host families were to be the core of our new social circles. We would take part in their get-togethers on occasions such as Christmas and Thanksgiving. Dodie and I were assigned to Kathleen and John Fisher and their family, and the morning after we arrived, Kathleen came by and picked us up at the Inn and took us to her home. It was clear from the get go that we had hit it off, and the relationship between our families developed from an academic program to a very close friendship that has endured throughout the years. Kathleen and John had five gorgeous kids, three boys and two girls. They graciously put us in their eldest son, Andy's, room for a couple of days until we got our own place. We spent a lot of the time sleeping, on account of the jet lag, and from time to time the kids would peek into our room in fascination at the strange people from so far away. I instantly fell in love with their youngest, Katie, who couldn't have been more than five at the time. I believe that the feeling was mutual, as Katie would always ask about me, preferring to refer to me as "you know who," a title that I grew to like because it came from the adorable Katie.

Kathleen spared no effort in making our transition as smooth as she possibly could, and along with her family she became an integral part of our life. We knew very early on that we had been extremely fortunate to make her acquaintance, and she had made our lives richer and warmer. Some people are blessed by the ability to bring joy into the lives of those they touch, and Kathleen is certainly one such person. I still remember how proud she was of us when we bought our first American car, a neat sporty Pontiac that carried us through graduate school. I sold it to a fellow graduate student only when I obtained my Ph.D. from Clemson and was about to move to Chicago to start my job.

The **Shah of Iran and President Jimmy Carter**

source: http://www.realclearpolitics.com/

Hossam, Katie and the Fisher Boys,
South Bend, Indiana, 1980

(Private collection)

Into the Eighties

I successfully completed the requirements for my Master's Degree in Civil Engineering from the University of Notre Dame in December of 1981, and although I loved Notre Dame and our friends from South Bend, my Middle Eastern body had had enough of the cruel winters of the Midwest. I applied to the doctoral program at Clemson University in South Carolina and was accepted. Aside from having a great reputation as an engineering school, the fact that it was a good 760 miles south of South Bend made it even more attractive to me. Dodie and I ended up spending the following three years in the small and quiet southern town of Clemson.

My doctoral advisor at Clemson was Professor Nelson Bauld, Jr., who I liked and admired tremendously. He was always helping me cut through the intricacies of my academic research and was a fine man indeed. I have seen him on numerous occasions sitting in his office before class preparing a lecture. I would ask him why he bothered with all this preparation despite the fact that he had given this lecture so many times before. Dr. Bauld would reply kindly with the warm smile that was so typical of him that even if it were not the first time for him to give that particular lecture, it was still the first time for this current group of students to hear it. I learned from this man that a good work ethic is not only an integral part of the educational process, but more importantly an essential part of self-esteem. So you can see that beyond his exceptional erudition, this man taught as much by example.

24

We had a great time at Clemson, and to understand how happy we were down there, you should know that during our stay we were blessed by the arrival of our first child, our son Omar, midway through our stay in Clemson. We were equally grateful for the services of his pediatrician, Dr. Gentry, who provided unparalleled care for Omar, and would check in with us by phone when Omar was not feeling well. He always acted as though he were one of the family. What a guy. Incidentally, Dr. Gentry was Jewish and fully appreciated the fact that our first born was a boy. I am telling you there are so many similarities—many more than there are differences— among people. If only we'd give ourselves a chance to listen to others and attempt to see the world through their eyes, there would be more compassion in this world to offset the fear. Or is that too much to hope for? Dr. Gentry, who provided so much care to Omar, would be proud to know that he too has become a physician.

At Clemson we lived in a duplex with our neighbors Rick, Randy and their little son George. Both were graduate students, and we had a good time together. In the summer of 1983, I underwent a minor surgical procedure in the nearby town of Anderson. I recall awakening from anesthesia in unbearable pain. So don't believe them when they tell you surgery can be minor. Believe me; if it's surgery, it is never minor. But I woke up to this horrible pain with Randy holding my hand and seeking to comfort me. Later on I was given some strong pain killers, and I managed to get through it. I still, however, cannot forget the kind touch of our dear Randy who decided to share with Dodie that tough duty of looking after a loved one recovering from surgery.

As I became friends with locals in and around Clemson, I was struck by something very odd in the Southern mindset. I got the feeling that some folks down there still thought that secession was a good idea which, unfortunately, had failed to materialize. To me this seemed odd on so many levels. Firstly, hadn't anyone told these folks that at that time the civil war had been a done deal for more than 120 years? Secondly, how could such a notion still persist in the hearts and minds of people who professed to be true patriotic Americans? Was it not tantamount to treason? Thirdly, even if in the unlikely scenario that were such a thing to happen at this late date, had anyone considered how badly they would fare as a result? Was this not plain absurd? Well, if you think that this was only a fluke, think again. Fast forward to 2012 and you will still hear that same hysterical cry uttered, this time by the politicians of some southern states. How sad is that? Is it not painfully obvious that the strength of this nation lies in the strength of its union? And does political dissent have the right to undermine the foundation of the democracy that we all cherish? When did it become OK to threaten violence in the face of adversity? Something is not right in this picture. Something that calls for the attention of sociopolitical experts—I must admit, this one has me stumped.

• •

I earned my doctoral degree in engineering in December 1984, and got a job right away in one of the major engineering firms in Chicago. Dodie, Omar, and I drove up for a couple of days, and we entered Chicago on January 4th 1985 amidst one foul blizzard. At times the snow was so intense that visibility was reduced to no more than a few feet. We parked on the shoulder repeatedly and, when driving was possible, we had to drive at no more than fifteen or twenty miles an hour for extended periods. In retrospect, I believe this was but a hint of what lay ahead for me.

You probably are aware of the feeling you get when you see someone for the first time and know even without exchanging a word that you would not under any circumstances get along with that person. Well, that's my own theory about places; they are just like people. You will either get along fine, or it will be just plain misery. Sadly, Chicago and I fell into the latter category. Murphy's Law kicked into high gear, I never liked the town, and she didn't hesitate to let me know how she felt about me. For nearly two years,

I held a job I did not like in a city I did not care for. One of my few good memories is that my second son Joey was born there.

It was during these couple of years that I realized that I was not cut out for the corporate world; I just could not adapt to doing things in a way that was dictated to me by someone else. It was just not me. All the engineers worked in a common open space where we were identified not by our names, but rather by our coordinates on the grid used to represent that space. That's how our interoffice mail was delivered to us. This may have been an efficient way to organize a workforce, but it was impersonal and made me feel so insignificant. I drew comparisons between my work there and Charlie Chaplin's portrayal of work on the assembly line in his 1936 silent movie, Modern Times. Remember how he used to stand in the same place all day tightening nuts as they whizzed by him on the fast-moving conveyor belt? Even during his breaks, the poor man would involuntarily continue the twitching motion even though he was no longer working. Was that a great movie or what? This genius recognized even back in 1936 the downside of the same industrial revolution that has done so much to improve the way we all live.

Hardy Campbell and I were best friends during my stay in Chicago. We would take our fifteen minute breaks together and complain about our misfortunes while sipping our coffee. He was an excellent structural engineer, but he could not stand the stifling routine any better than me. Not wanting to waste our entire fifteen minutes talking about our misery, he would quickly change the topic to his lovely home town of San Diego. As we sat next to the window that made us all too aware of the weather that awaited us at the end of our shift, he would tell me about San Diego in so much detail and with so much love that almost made me believe that it was the most beautiful place on earth. One day I told him that we were like two teen aged boys sharing feelings about a girl; I had fallen in love with his San Diego sight unseen! By the way, it took me all of twenty five years to lay eyes on her beauty. It was only in the summer of 2009 that I had the opportunity to visit San Diego for the first time. It is just as lovely today as Hardy said it was back then. However, I'm from the Bay Area, and you probably know where I left my heart prior to that departure for Southern California.

The 80's were the Reagan years. As a two term president, he revolutionized the economic culture in Washington and in the nation. True to his Republican ideals, he came up with this philosophy of trickledown economics. The Rich were given tax cuts that were supposed to stimulate the economy through the creation of more jobs for everybody else. The problem with this fancy notion was that while the part about tax cuts did materialize, the same was never true for the part about trickledown. Those who benefitted from these policies simply lined their pockets with the freebies and never looked back to see how the rest of the nation was doing. Another idea that was brought to practice by this nice man was deregulation, deregulation, and more deregulation. In an infamous one liner—a trait for which he was famous—Reagan proclaimed that government was not the solution to our problems, government was itself the problem. This sounded nice on TV, but it was simply a fallacy. Reagan's mantra became the Republican doctrine for the next twenty years, and his words were taken as scripture. I would not be surprised if these words were carved in stone and enshrined somewhere in the archives of the Republican Party. It took more than twenty years to realize how ridiculous these policies were. It wasn't until the fall of 2008 that the real consequences of such blabber came through like flood waters bursting the dam that had held them back for so long. The results were an economic failure similar in its gravity to the Great Depression. And now, it seems that there may be no solution to the problem but government! What a paradox! So much for trickledown economics, and so much for market deregulation. Goodbye to sound bites and bad philosophy!

29

The Iran- Contra fiasco was yet another massive blunder from which Reagan managed to escape unscathed. Somehow, a fall guy in the name of Oliver North shielded the president. The scandal was that deals had been struck with the Iranians to facilitate the release of six American hostages held by Hezbollah in exchange for the provision of arms to Iran. A further strategic goal was to use the funds from the arms deal to illegally fund the Contras of Nicaragua in their fight against the communist Sandinistas. The problem with this fancy foot work was that they were breaking the law on both sides of the world. Not only was arming the Contras illegal, there was also an arms embargo in place at the time against Iran. Furthermore, when exposed the deal became a foreign policy debacle putting the administration in an unenviable, embarrassing, and awkward position. Even though there was never a direct link established between these events and Ronald Reagan himself, one can't but wonder why this fiasco did not lead to a huge international scandal as weighty as Watergate was for Nixon. Moreover, why was Nixon disgraced, while Reagan was glamorized? Funny is this business of politics, isn't it?

30

Let's draw one more time from the well of Herodotus and reflect upon what the great historian said about men and circumstances. There was Reagan, making his great speeches against the evil empire—a reference to the now defunct Soviet Union–and then being credited for its actual collapse, despite the fact that the Soviet empire imploded from its own internal problems. The exact same story is told about Ronald Reagan and the collapse of the Berlin Wall. However, just because you call for something to happen, that does not mean you actually brought it about when it comes to pass. As in Hollywood, sometimes it's just good timing. Yet, many people still give him credit for these events. Like everybody else, some presidents seem to have better stars than others.

Let's just say that Ronald Reagan as president deserves no better a grade than he did as an actor. History may regard his presidency as having even less merit than his movies.

The Nineties

The Nineties belonged to the man from Little Rock, Arkansas. And just as a side note, let me say that some presidents have been skipped in this chronology for no better reason than my unprofessional opinion that their presidencies were either uneventful or even lackluster. My own lack of interest in the presidencies of Gerald Ford and George H. W. Bush is to be blamed for them being dropped from this outline.

A master politician if there was ever one, Bill Clinton managed to lead the country to one of its most prosperous decades in recent history. He assembled a White House team that was up to the task and implemented his policies to a tee. Not only did he lay the foundation for strong growth and job creation at home, he also tackled some of the more difficult foreign policy challenges and did so quite successfully. His efforts in the Middle East led to the Oslo agreement, a blueprint for peace between the Palestinians and the Israelis that probably would have worked out if only he had been able to maintain the political momentum to propel it forwards after the initial success. Unfortunately, this momentum was lost when he was dragged into a political dog fight over his relations with the Whitehouse intern, Monica Lewinsky. This debacle consumed so much of his energies for the balance of his presidency. On a different front he championed political and even military efforts to deal with the Bosnian problem, a matter of ethnic cleansing in Europe, of all places! Such efforts ultimately resulted in the ousting of the Yugoslav dictator, Slobodan Milosevic. This tyrant was brought to trial as a war criminal at The Hague and was sent to his fate. He died in prison before the judicial process was complete. Is Europe and along with it the rest of the world better off without him? Absolutely.

As a result of Clinton's masterful leadership the economy flourished, the deficit diminished, and things looked as good as could be. That is of course until we became aware of the inner demons he struggled with— and we all have our own struggles throughout our lives. We win some, we lose some. So he liked the ladies, and when caught with his pants down–please pardon the pun—he did what any married man in his right mind would do. He lied! Show me a man who would not lie under similar circumstances, and I'll show you someone too dumb for his own good. However the evaluation of this indiscretion was put into perspective by the president who succeeded him. Recall how after W's invasion of Iraq those bumper stickers that proclaimed "When Clinton lied, no one died."

How true is that? Indeed Clinton was guilty of a transgression that cost him most of his political capital and led to his impeachment, but did his actions really warrant all the fuss? Again we are faced with a situation where politicians manipulate circumstances for their own political gain without regard for the bigger picture. Clinton was doing a good job in the Whitehouse, and the country would have been better off were he not dragged into this ugly street fight. He would have continued his good work for the benefit of all Americans. And again, please understand that I do not condone infidelity—I vehemently do not. My point is simply that this was a matter better left to those individuals who were personally affected. In other words, family matters are best handled by family members, and should preferably be resolved confidentially by two or, at most, three people.

What is it about Americans that time and again gets them sucked into this dubious sense of righteousness when it comes to their leaders? If I want to talk about politicians and their flings, I'd very likely have enough material for a whole series of very interesting books. And, when it comes to casting first stones about the marital relationships of our presidents, we should think very carefully before we do so. And we should think again, because a very large segment of our population would probably be injured in the crossfire. Come on now, get real. Clinton was a brilliant president whose inner demons caught up with him and cost him dearly.

Due to health issues and other work engagements, Clinton dropped from the public eye after he left the White House. A few years later he underwent heart surgery to treat the damage done by his many years of junk food consumption, especially those industrial strength burgers he loved so much. It was only late in W's presidency before I was once again able to see Bill back in action on a late night TV show. I sat mesmerized; the man's brilliance is simply amazing. It is hard for me to imagine that anyone could be so thoughtful and have so much insight about every topic thrown at him. As the interview concluded, I found myself turning to Dodie and saying, "Did you see that? This man speaks in thought-filled, idea-dense entire paragraphs, as opposed to what we've been witnessing for the past eight years." You will recall that his replacement was somebody who invariably began sentences without ever managing to end them, and was so unintelligible that it is a wonder that he ever became the American president. The difference in IQ between these two characters is no doubt proportionate to the difference between the massive surplus left by the former and the even more massive deficit with which the latter had saddled the rest of us.

The Elephant in the Room

So here we are, having to finally acknowledge the elephant in the room. This is the one topic I must now finally confront. I am talking of course about the Israeli-Palestinian conflict. Peace in the Middle East and the rest of the world may very well depend on the resolution of this problem. But what are its origins, and what makes it hard to resolve? For insight into these matters, we need a brief discussion of the historical background. So here goes.

Remnants of the family of Jacob, the son of Isaac and a descendant of Abraham, migrated to Palestine. The Bible tells us there were about 70 of them. Their descendants again migrated at around 1650 BC, this time to Egypt, where they remained until their exodus centuries later, after which they spent forty years wandering in the Sinai desert. After this, these followers of Moses, the 12 tribes that descended from the sons of Jacob, showed up again in Palestine between 1200-1000 BC and numerous skirmishes took place with the Palestinians. In about 1010 BC, David became the leader of the Jews and he spent some fifteen years attempting to reconcile the feuding Jewish tribes, especially among the Jehovah and the Benjamin tribes. The final reconciliation took place in 997 BC. The next few years were used by David to build up his nation, while capitalizing on the weakened state of the Palestinians who had become disunited. At that time the Kanans were preoccupied by their trade activities, whereas the Ashourians' powers were weakening. Taking advantage of the disorganized state of his adversaries, David solidified his presence by occupying large parts of Al-Sham (corresponding loosely to modern day Syria.) During the reign of his son Solomon, however, most of these occupied territories were liberated.

It is important to note that, on a different front, the Babylonians were worried about their trade lines to India via Persia. Thus merchants thought of utilizing an alternate maritime route to and from India through the Arabian Sea towards Yemen, and from there through the Red Sea to the Strait of Aqaba towards Al-Sham and Iraq. Needless to say, the Israelites attempted to make that goal unattainable for their adversaries, the Babylonians, in an attempt to stifle their trading routes in order to weaken them further.

It is, therefore, safe to conclude that the Jewish presence in Palestine and Al-Sham was never fully developed due to the influence of the strong rivaling powers of the Pharaohs of Egypt on one hand, and the Ashourians on the other.

40

Now let's leave behind biblical times and move on to more recent history; specifically that of the twentieth century.

In 1917, the British government decided to endorse the establishment of a Jewish state in Palestine through what was known as the Balfour Declaration. The actual implementation of this declaration materialized towards the end of WWII, and in 1947 the UN adopted a partitioning plan that divided Palestine into two states, an Arab state and a Jewish one. In 1948, war broke out between the Arabs and the Jews. The outcome of this war was the defeat of the Arab forces and the establishment of the state of Israel. Since that time, the Arabs and the Jews have engaged in three more wars. The first was in 1956 when troops of England, France, and Israel invaded Egypt in response to the Egyptian nationalization of the Suez Canal, which connects the Far East to the Middle East and Europe. That invasion was repulsed, and the invading forces withdrew due to the worldwide condemnation of their actions. To a great extent, world opinion was led by the American president, Dwight D. Eisenhower. At that time, Egypt was a young republic, no more than four years of age, and American diplomacy sought to establish a positive rapport with its new leader, President Nasser. This would prove to be the first and only time that the United States sided with an Arab nation against Israel. At the time, Nasser declared the withdrawal of the invading forces a political victory.

41

The next military confrontation was in 1967 in what became known as the six-day-war, whereas noted previously; the Arab forces were soundly defeated. Following this war came the 1973 war which resulted in Egypt's recovery of all territory lost as a result of the previous war. At the time of this writing, the peace treaty is still in effect between the Egyptians and the Israelis, a treaty made possible by President Carter's 1978 Camp David Accords and signed at the Whitehouse by Anwar Sadat and Menachem Begin in 1979.

So what is the hurdling block in this whole situation? Well, it is simply that the Jewish people have managed to solve their homeland problem, but only by transferring it to the Palestinians who found themselves as a consequence a people without a nation. Not only that, apart from the Arab nations, which have strong cultural, historic, and religious ties with them, they were left without anyone to back their rightful demand for their own Palestinian land. No one else in the world seemed to care. Even with countless UN resolutions denouncing occupation by force, and urging the return of all such territories to their rightful owners, the reality on the ground is completely different, and the world has turned a deaf ear to this problem.

Palestinians live in tent cities without hope of any real opportunity to lead peaceful lives with their neighbors in Israel, while the Israelis mistrust the Arabs and continue to confiscate whatever land that remained in Palestinian hands. Such practices are justified by Israeli claims that the Arabs want to destroy the Jewish state, and these actions are justified in the name of self-defense. Such arguments may sound fair on the surface, but checked against the realities of everyday life, the fallacies become apparent. Jimmy Carter's book, *Palestine: Peace Not Apartheid* presents a view by a fair and neutral observer of the inhumane practices suffered by these people on a daily basis.

A significant amount of bad blood exists between these parties, which in turn compounds the difficulty of reconciliation. I would be skeptical about any meaningful, long lasting resolution of this issue any time soon. Having said this, let me present a formula that may work. In a nut shell, it is a two state solution, in which Israel relinquishes land in return for the guarantee of a peaceful coexistence. This is obviously easier said than done, but the fact is that neither the Israelis nor the Palestinians are going anywhere in the foreseeable future; consequently, it only makes sense to work towards peace based on this recognition. For such a solution to even have the faintest hope of success, however, the United States must once again play the role of the just and impartial super power.

A strange paradox concerning the relations of the United States to the Arab World becomes apparent when one considers how favorably Americans have been perceived in the Mid-East as opposed to how strongly their governments have been denounced over the years. This paradox is really quite easy to explain away. The average American will always be able find his or her way to the hearts of ordinary people in any Arab country in part because the ordinary American is a kind-hearted, decent individual, full of love for life, and possessing a disposition that is admired by most people. Well, what about his government then? Here you run into trouble as a result of the skewed political stands that the US takes in the Mid-East. A judge who can always be counted on to favor a particular litigant quickly loses credibility. Regardless of the givens of a case, such a judge will invariably rule for the one side against the other. This precisely explains the paradox. Arabs are aware that while the US is the best equipped nation to act as a peace broker, they also know that it can't be counted on as a fair broker due to its bias over the past half century. Consider the UN resolutions in which the entire world would take a stand against some indisputable Israeli transgression, only to be vetoed by the US. This can hardly be called impartial.

What About Iran?

Iran is historically deep, culturally rich, and it has several millennia of experience in international politics and diplomacy. They pretty much invented the game. Furthermore, over the ages the Iranians have managed to maintain their foothold in one of the most precarious spots in the world. Iran has dealt with enemies left and right. They fought Alexander of Macedon in the fourth century BC, and in the first century AD; they battled a Roman Empire that was no longer content to merely rule the Mediterranean. The Romans were ready to take on the Persian Empire, the only other super power of the time. After this on-and-off struggle took place, the Iranians had to deal with the emergence of a new religion in the Arabian Desert, a religion committed to delivering its message to peoples and lands throughout the world. Islam indeed did find a fertile soil in the Persian Empire, and a large portion of the population adopted the new religion. Some of the most noted Islamic heroes and scholars are in fact of Persian descent. The Persians also had to take into account dangers from the east.

Central Asia was always a place where serious troubles might erupt. Nonetheless, throughout their long history the Persians still managed to keep trade lines open and communication flowing, which is a testament to their strategic and diplomatic skill and agility.

So what happened in recent years? In 1951 to the dismay of Britain and the West, the Iranians nationalized their oil industry. Up to this point, the British were the prime beneficiaries of Iranian oil, so following this act of national sovereignty, they orchestrated an economic boycott, and they also sought the support from the United States. In 1953 the CIA staged a coup against the democratically elected prime minister of Iran, Muhammad Mussadeq, and he was replaced by a titular monarch, the pro-western dictator, Shah Reza Pahlavi. This CIA effort, code named "Operation Ajax," has the dubious distinction of being the first covert American operation to overthrow a foreign government. The Shah returned the favor by dividing Iran's oil revenues evenly between the United States and the British, with the small remaining portion going to Iran. The status quo was maintained until 1979 when the Shah was ousted by the Iranian revolution and the emergence of Ayatollah Khomeini. We now have the Islamic Republic of Iran. It may be argued that the coup of 1953 was the instigator of the Islamic revolution that took place a quarter of a century later. Operation Ajax was not publically acknowledged until 2009 when Obama spelled out America's role in a famous and historic speech he delivered in Cairo, Egypt. However, the blowback from this subversion of a secular, democratic government has already outlasted whatever lesser benefits may have been gained during the Shah's dictatorship which was overthrown by the Islamic revolution.

As a sad footnote, the last days in the Shah's life were spent on his private plane flying all over the world trying to secure a place that would accept him as a refugee in the last stages of his terminal illness. No one extended a hand to this man except Sadat, who took him in where he remained until he died shortly thereafter. He is buried in Egypt.

In 1980 Saddam Hussein decided to invade Iran, and the Americans supplied him with arms as has been memorialized in that infamous photo of Saddam and Donald Rumsfeld locked in a firm handshake, evidence that leaves no doubt in the Iranians' minds as to where we stood in this fight. This war lasted a grueling eight years depleting the resources of both nations and ending in a deadlock without the slightest benefit for either side.

In more recent years, Iran was classified by W. as the center of his "The Axis of Evil," which stretched incongruously from North Korea to Iraq. Currently, the United States is spearheading an international campaign to stifle the Iranian nuclear program through sanctions and punitive measures.

So why don't these Iranians like us very much? Really?! Seriously now, how do we deal with Iran? There is no easy answer to this question, but let's try anyway. For starters, why don't we come to the table with an open mind and a willingness to treat them as the reputable nation with over 3,000 years of civilization? Approach them in a way that seeks reconciliation rather than confrontation, and communication rather than reprimand. Start out on a common ground and carefully work your way through the rough patches. In all likelihood many issues will find easy resolution, although others may end up requiring much greater patience and perseverance. Long-term goals have to be identified clearly so that everybody can stay on the same page. Avoid the typical political pitfall of discrediting all previous efforts by preceding administrations, which necessitates starting from scratch every time there is a change in administration. Foreign policy has to be dealt in a steady-handed and consistent manner. And what about the Iranian people, how do you go about addressing them? Well, you'd be surprised as to how favorable a view these folks have about the United States. You need to attempt the practice that is typically called winning the hearts and minds of a people, a proposition that is easily understood, but rarely implemented properly. If what we've been doing didn't work out in the past, doesn't it make sense to try something different? Or do we want to fall under Einstein's famous definition of madness by ceaselessly repeating the same thing while expecting different results? Can't we just realize that the world will invariably see us in a much better light when we extend a helping hand as opposed to when we are acting as a bully? This worked very well for America after the Second World War. Also, bear in mind that Iran has very strong ties and common interests with both Russia and China among others, a fact that should be considered when politicking or playing

50

hard ball. This might even put them in the very paradoxical position of effecting peace between these three superpowers if we encourage them.

In December 2004 a tsunami hit eleven countries bordering the Indian Ocean with a violent tidal wave 100 feet high resulting in 230,000 deaths in addition to the physical devastation it left behind. Take a look at the world's reaction following this horrendous tragedy. The entire world was indebted to the United States for its leading role in helping those affected by this ordeal. The bang for buck we got from this humanitarian action makes it indisputable that kind acts will always carry you much further than other approaches along the path of human interaction. Nothing else even comes close. Just try it.

51

• •

Donald Rumsfeld and Saddam Hussein

http://www.xmfan.com/viewtopic.php?t=27461

Afghanistan

As far back as the early Fourth Century BC, Alexander the Great invaded Afghanistan and Persia and added both to his empire. His control, however, did not last for long, and following his death in 323BC, the Greeks' grip over the country started to loosen in part due to feuding among his generals.

By 642 AD the Arabs had completed their invasion of Persia and Afghanistan. (The Islamic and Persian influence on Afghanistan proved to be the most dominant and most lasting through the subsequent years.) In the thirteenth century, Genghis Khan invaded the country but never managed to rid it of the Islamic influence; in fact two of his successors converted.

To witness the European influence on Afghanistan, we have to fast forward to the early 19th century during which the British and Russians had a power struggle over the crossroads of central Asia. In WWI, Afghanistan took a neutral stand despite the anti-British sentiment that was prevalent at that time.

On Christmas day 1979, the Soviet troops entered Kabul signaling the start of a war that will last through early 1989 when the Soviets withdrew completely from the country thanks to the massive support provided to the Mujahedeen by the CIA and the Saudis. It was in 1988 that Osama Bin Laden had formally established Al-Qaeda to fight against the Russians in Afghanistan and probably elsewhere as well. And you know what they say about politics and strange bed fellows. Well that is exactly what had transpired in the collaboration between the CIA and Bin Laden during those years. The CIA would rather forget about this relationship in light of what took place down the line.

Following the events of September 11th, 2001, and the Taliban's refusal to cooperate with the United States in bringing to justice the Al-Qaeda elements that conspired in that attack on the World Trade Center, the Bush administration invaded Afghanistan and targeted Al-Qaeda strong points. Yet Bush did not succeed in capturing Bin Laden who managed to escape to the mountainous regions along the border with Pakistan, an area even more rugged than the rest of Afghanistan. Sometimes geography proves to be one's worst enemy. Afghanistan is a nation with minimal infrastructure and has an extremely tough terrain to traverse. However, this is no problem to people whose lifestyle is many centuries behind that of the industrialized world. And if this did not by itself present enough difficulties, throw into the mix yet another factor that makes things even worse: the fact that over 90% of all the opium in the world comes from this very spot. Not surprisingly, the annual drug revenue is estimated at $64 billion, a good chunk of change that I suspect most people would fight very hard for.

The mission of tracking Al-Qaeda elements was inexplicably abandoned by W's administration, and focus turned to the invasion of Iraq in the spring of 2003: an invasion that proved very costly to Americans who still suffer from its aftermath. I will discuss this debacle a little bit later. For now, suffice it to say that dropping the ball in Afghanistan resulted in horrible repercussions, not the least of which is the resurgence of the Taliban factions which had been on the run for many years before that. At the present time, the Taliban influence in Afghanistan is stronger than it ever was, and we're back to square one thanks to the policies of W.

President Obama opines that since Afghanistan is indeed the hot spot in this conflict, it is therefore imperative that we focus all our attention and resources including military on that nation, instead of on Iraq, a nation that had nothing to do with the aforementioned events. Obama takes the stand that we should reduce our troop levels in Iraq until we reach a reasonable departure point, whereas we should conversely increase those in Afghanistan. I believe that only half of his conclusion is correct. Again there is no other way in Iraq but out. As for Afghanistan, I think that the political leadership will eventually reach the same conclusion that it has reached in the case of Iraq. The difficulty of fighting such a war in this "graveyard of empires" has been described poignantly by one military expert who refused to justify wasting tens of thousands of dollars in military strikes that target ten dollar tents somewhere in a desert. This and similar arguments elucidate a dilemma that is not easily resolved. You know you have an enemy hiding in those mountains, yet your regular armed forces are not the right tool for the job. Isn't it time to look for better ways of handling this mess? Or are we behaving like someone whose only tool is a hammer and sees all problems as nails? Maybe now it's time for a different approach and, indeed, a different tool. What about covert operations that do not require the deployment of hundreds of thousands of troops to fight a guerrilla war that cannot be won? I'm told there are people in Langley who are quite well versed in the business. Maybe it is time to give the job to them.

The Afghani terrain is not going to change, it will always be an almost uninvadable country, nor will its people's lifestyle, at least not in the foreseeable future. If such a change is to occur, it will only come about by the enlightenment of the new generations through education and by convincing them by example that the western world is not out to get them. We must persuade them that we are not the monster they imagine us to be. Furthermore, drug trafficking will continue to take place in this nation simply because of the obscene profits it offers. Let's learn from past experiences dealing with similar problems. How did we fight the drug war in Colombia for example? It is to be understood that there are going to be differences in some of the details, but let's adopt the techniques that have proven effective with the necessary modifications. In the case of Colombia, the United States had utilized independent contractors to work in unison with the Colombian government in an effort to try to eradicate coca production. This along with cutting off US aid proved to be a working formula in this ongoing struggle. The current problem, however, is compounded by the fact that the government of Hamid Karzai does not have full control of the country; in fact drug lords still control major parts of this unfortunate nation. Perhaps intercepting trafficking lines and heavy sentences for convicted drug traffickers will be effective. This, however, must be a concerted effort that is backed by the good will of the international community to avoid the perception of unilateral action; a reputation that has stuck to the US in recent years.

Bin Laden

The period between the end of WWII and the collapse of the former Soviet Union is generally referred to as the Cold War years. Both the United States and the Soviet Union were involved in a military power struggle that fell short of a shooting war, but covered just about every corner of the planet. Some of the more famous examples of the manifestation of this Cold War included the Bay of Pigs and the Cuban Missile Crisis during the presidency of JFK. These confrontations during the Kennedy Administration were serious enough to bring the world—for the first time ever— to the brink of a nuclear war which could have engulfed the entire planet. This fate was averted at the last moment through tense and difficult diplomatic efforts. In Europe during this period, the world also witnessed the events that took place in Hungary in 1956 and the former Czechoslovakia in 1968. On both occasions resistance to a Soviet client regime was brutally crushed by the Soviet military, and these reprisals sent a clear message to the rest of the world that the Soviet Union would stand very tough in defense of the strategic interests it had acquired as a victorious party in WWII.

So what does any of that have to do with Bin Laden, for goodness sake? Well, fast forward to Christmas Eve of 1979 when the Soviets invaded Afghanistan to provide necessary support to their client communist governing regime against the Islamic Mujahideen. The latter group was supported by the United States and other western nations as well as by numerous Arab nations, notably Saudi Arabia, Egypt and others. This planted the seeds that eventually mushroomed to what we today call international terrorism!

In an attempt to undermine the Soviet position in Afghanistan, the United States had aligned itself with the Mujahideen by providing extensive guerilla warfare training and financial support through the CIA. Well, the training and support worked fine in that the Mujahideen managed, over a period of about nine years, to create untenable conditions for the Soviets, and these fighters were every bit as rough and tough as the Afghani terrain itself. In the end, the Soviets pulled out of Afghanistan in the middle of February 1989 leaving behind a legacy of their own Vietnam!

You know what they say about a player dropping the ball and how disappointing the consequences of such actions are. Think of our subsequent policy in Afghanistan as doing just that. The point is that those same Mujahideen were completely ignored after they fulfilled their role in expelling the Russians, and no one wanted to be associated with them any longer. As is often the case, the devil is in the details, as was indeed the case here. We had left behind to roam freely a highly trained and battle-tested group of individuals, but we had no idea about what their actual alliances were. As it turns out, a bunch of zealous young men associated with those folks ended up flying two planes into the World Trade Center, murdering thousands of innocent civilians, and changing forever the character of our national defense. Today we are living in a world of asymmetrical conflicts where formal armed units are tasked with fighting terrorists who can pop up anywhere in the world and, when successful, hit whatever target they choose. As noted earlier, this is not the scenario best suited to conventional military maneuvers.

While the goal of preventing terrorism is noble, we cannot hope to succeed until the problem is handled by the entire world in a completely different way. Note that this is not a problem that faces just a few nations; it is indeed a universal problem. Take a look at some of the terrorist attacks that have taken place in recent times to validate this fact. Some of these attacks have taken place during the last two decades in the land of the Pharaohs, where extremism finds fertile soil. Poor socioeconomic conditions have prevailed in Egypt for a long time, and coupled with the religious zeal that can be manipulated under such circumstances, it is not hard to see why this terrorism occurred there. The targets were again innocent civilians, mostly European tourists vacationing in one of the most fascinating places on earth. These unsuspecting tourists would find their tour buses exploding or ambushed by gunmen for no reason

61

whatsoever. Needless to say, it took only a couple of these attacks to bring tourism, one of the major industries in Egypt, to its knees, as the clientele immediately found other much safer retreats. This all happened in the mid-nineties and the country suffered serious economic losses. These losses were in fact the unstated purpose behind these cowardly acts. The terrorism was an attempt to cripple the government and make a bad situation far worse. The regime reacted very forcefully, and the parties responsible were tracked down and were swiftly brought to justice. The damage, however, had already been done. At the time, the Egyptian president, Hosni Mubarak, pleaded for the world's support in fighting this very difficult battle, but no one listened to him. The rationalization then was that such events were happening on account of human rights violations in that nation. Yet, although such violations existed then and maybe still are lingering to this day, they were not the driving force for these acts. The false sense of security within the western world would be shattered on September 11, 2001.

In more recent times, in the spring of 2004, only a few days following the Spanish general elections, a series of explosions rocked the Spanish capital as bombs exploded in a number of commuter trains during the morning rush hour. A couple of hundred people lost their lives while a couple of thousand more sustained injuries. The perpetrators were Al-Qaeda sympathizers.

Another almost identical plan was carried out in the summer of 2005 by suicide bombers, this time on London's mass transport system, again during the morning commute. More than fifty people were killed and about 700 were wounded. One disturbing fact about these attacks was that the bombers were British citizens, a distinction with far reaching implications and one that complicates this battle even further. Not only must nations be on the lookout for foreign enemies, they now have to be on the watch for terrorist cells springing up among their own people. What a mess.

So what can be done in light of these new realities? Well, as is the case with any problem, the first step towards solving it is to correctly and clearly identify the problem. We then must devise solutions that fit these clearly defined parameters. The following step is to gather international support and ensure that every nation is fully aware of this danger and, consequently, prepared to participate fully and actively in coordinated efforts. The final stage is the forceful implementation of these measures through a worldwide collaborative action plan.

This list may appear quite cut and dried, implying perhaps that following a set of instructions would guarantee success. That is certainly not the impression I wish to leave you with. To get a clearer picture, let's visit the solution algorithm one more time—only now we will need to pay closer attention to the nuts and bolts.

As a lecturer in Mathematics, I emphasize to my students the importance of clear and precise definitions for any given setup. This insistence on the particulars might seem to them excessive, but I believe that such a degree of detail is needed to preclude any misgivings or misconceptions of the issues in play. And real life is no exception. Take a look at many real life situations that fall apart simply because the different parties involved operate from different understandings of the common terminology. How many feuds might be avoided if people would define their terms and agree on these definitions beforehand? With this in mind, let's begin by defining the problem. Who is the culprit here? What is creating all this mess? Is it Islam the religion, is it Muslims at large, or is it a small peripheral group?

64

As a well-informed Muslim, I can tell you that there is just nothing wrong with the religion of Islam. The truth of the matter is that the Arabic words for both Islam and peace share the same linguistic root! Take a look at the word "Islam" and the word "Salam" to easily see the point. The former is the name of the religion, whereas the latter is the Arabic word for peace. See how closely related this word is to its Hebrew equivalent, "Shalom." Did I not tell you that we are all much closer to one another than we often realize? Like its Jewish and Christian precursors, all of which are biblical religions and consequently, "of the book," Islam is a religion that cherishes peaceful coexistence with everybody and peace on earth. Is it any surprise that this very message is one that has resonated through all three of these religions, and indeed all world religions? Do not all religions emerge from the same source? Do they not all derive from and point to the same creator? If so, it only stands to reason that the core of all religions would be essentially the same. Can you find a religion with directives that are not in harmony with the golden rule or the Ten Commandments? Is there a religion that gives a nod to killing, stealing, and adultery? How is it then that we get ourselves into arguments about the inevitability of the clash between religions? The holy Quran states in one of its verses that we were created from a man and a woman and formed into nations and tribes so that we can get to know one another. This is the reality of Islam. So we can conclude that the problem does not lie in the religion.

How about the Muslims themselves? Could it be that this is where the problem exists? Well, as followers of a religion that advocates mutual respect and tolerance, it is not hard to realize that Muslims as a whole yearn for a peaceful coexistence with everybody else on earth as much as everyone else does. Across the board, you are most likely to encounter Muslims who are God-fearing, hard-working, and peace-loving folks with hopes and aspirations no different from those of anyone else.

As you can see, we are left with one remaining culprit, and that is the small, peripheral groups that use the good name of a peaceful religion to justify heinous crimes that can never be condoned by the doctrines of Islam. Who are these people, you might then ask?

The truth of the matter is that in all faiths, one will find extremists who will raise the flag of religion while carrying out an agenda that is rarely religious. There are many actual motives for such extremism which often involve political, economic, and social considerations. An example of this was noted earlier when addressing the Iranian Revolution of Khomeini. In that case, the good name of Islam was abused in order to disguise a simple political power grab. In the case of Bin Laden, on the other hand, the reasons are more obscure. This is because Bin Laden devised his message to resonate with simple-minded, zealous youngsters. His skillful handling of the intricacies of the contemporary situation allowed him to portray himself as a worldwide spokesman for and defender of Islam. The formula is essentially a straightforward one that appeals to the dismay that Arabs feel towards the west for the biased stand on the Israeli-Palestinian problem and add to this feeling the dissatisfaction of the Arab populace with their own political and economic conditions. Under these circumstances, all one needs to do is to fuel the already existing anger, and offer an alternative that appears to be religious and promises to regain their lost national pride. Nonetheless, this camouflage never fooled anyone in their right mind, and many immediately saw Bin Laden for what he was. Within his family circle, Bin Laden was shunned and even denounced, while on a national level, he was banished and his Saudi citizenship revoked. It was clear then, and it is now clear to just about every Muslim that he was nothing but a dangerous man who did much more harm than good, and that what he preached had nothing to do with the teachings of the great religion of Islam. In the eyes of millions of Muslims, he is no different from Carlos the Jackal, the infamous seventies terrorist.

The message of Bin Laden does not stand to any serious scrutiny, as evidenced in yet another conflict: the current Iraq war. In the early stages of this conflict, Al-Qaeda leadership thought it would be able to carry through its plans, and it appeared for a time that it was indeed succeeding. Following the overthrow of the Saddam regime, Al-Qaeda gained a foothold in Iraq, and was a thorn in the side of the coalition forces. However, when the Iraqi people themselves learned from experience the harm these zealots could cause them, their influence diminished, and they ceased to be a factor in what had been considered a fertile ground for their movement. No one in Iraq was fooled by the claim that the American occupation occurred for their liberation, and no one there was deceived for long by Al-Qaeda.

One can safely conclude then that the real culprits in this era of international terrorism are none other than a marginal group of extremists who represent no one but themselves and who serve no purpose except their own. They are to be viewed for what they are, anarchists who must be dealt with through a unified world that seeks peace and prosperity for all mankind.

It may seem farfetched that the wars against terrorism and drugs have a strong correlation, but the truth is that they certainly do. In each of these cases, there are attempts to carry out illegal activities, and in each case no success can be assured without full international collaboration. The sad reality is, however, that neither activity can be dealt a knockout punch or terminated once and for all. Just as one can never prevent a new poppy seed from sprouting in a field somewhere halfway around the world, one cannot prevent a naïve youngster from being recruited to take part in a "holy war." Let us brace ourselves for a sustained and continuous fight against terrorism, as we did some time ago in the case of drug trafficking. Problems with terrorism and illegal drugs will remain throughout our lifetime, and, unfortunately the lives of our children. It makes sense, therefore, to utilize those lessons learned from the sustained war against drugs for use against terrorism. It is indeed harder to control the seed than it is to control its spreading around the world. This is where all efforts must focus to ensure a strong quarantine against the spread of this disease. We need to always be on the watch for those new fields for growing terrorists, and they are not hard to predict. We simply need to be alert to the world around us. A good first place to look would be those areas which remain in the middle ages and refuse to join the modern world. Be on the lookout for places that are tied to existing beds of terrorism. For example, although Afghanistan was the center of planning for the 2001 attacks, it would be ludicrous to ignore the strong ties between this nation and its neighboring Pakistan. Political analysts agree today that the latter nation is indeed where attention should be given, and that it is indeed a more complex proposition than the former due to its favorable relations with the Western world in general and the United States in particular. Nonetheless, Pakistan is a far more difficult problem to solve because in addition to the above mentioned factors, it is a nation that tries to play by the rules and one that strives to honor democratic values. Lastly, let's not forget that it is one of the few nations that possess nuclear weapons. Needless to say, this is a reality that must never be overlooked!

Osama Bin Laden

http://www.fifthinternationale.com/robots/osama.html

Iraq

I will skip the historical background presented in the preceding cases, not because it is uninteresting, but only because the recent events are much more worthy of mentioning in the context of this discussion.

In August 1990, Saddam Hussein decided to invade neighboring Kuwait and declare it a part of Iraq. The trigger of this action was twofold; one is the fact that the Iraqi leadership was frustrated by the insufficient financial support offered by this wealthy neighbor, despite its massive financial losses resulting from the eight year war with Iran. At the time, Saddam believed that he was carrying the torch of defending Kuwait and the Gulf nations against the Persian tide. He, therefore, was fully convinced that it was these nations' duty to foot the bill for his war. Whether his belief was entirely true is debatable; here, we are simply putting ourselves in his shoes in an attempt to understand why he acted the way he did. In addition to this, upon gaining control over the much militarily weaker Kuwait, consider how he declared the outcome. He did not say that he was claiming Kuwait, but rather that it had become the 19th Iraqi province. Saddam like other Iraqis was indeed convinced that Kuwait was a historical and geographical part of the Iraqi territorial claim, and it ought to be regarded as such by everyone else; and the Iraqis had their own evidence to support these claims. Bear in mind that we are talking about national entities that date back no earlier than the post WWI era when their political boundaries were drawn following the defeat of the Ottoman Empire by the British. Furthermore, a cursory look at the map of the region will indicate how Kuwait was arbitrarily separated from the much larger territory of Iraq itself. Let me reemphasize that the reasoning just provided is by no means a justification of what took place in the summer of 1990, but only part of an attempt to understand Saddam's motives.

For reasons that never became clear, Saddam believed that his move would be tolerated by the Americans, although one cause might have been that he misconstrued the American ambassador's position as a signal by the US that it would look the other way if he did in fact invade. He also seems to have gained confidence from his belief that the Americans would not meaningfully retaliate because of the logistical difficulties involved in the exercise of any military option. To his surprise and great dismay, he was faced with one of the most powerful international coalitions, and Operation Desert Storm commenced at the beginning of 1991. Multinational forces gathered into the region bent upon liberating Kuwait and forcing the Iraqi army to pull out. This goal was accomplished with the blessing of nearly the entire world.

Following Saddam's defeat, the international community applied economic sanctions against Iraq as well as a close monitoring system approved by the UN in order to ensure that Iraq did not increase its military capacity or threaten its neighbors again. These sanctions remained in place throughout the nineties, with frequent UN inspections. A no-fly zone was also imposed on the Iraqi air force, and Saddam was kept in check. At the time the US decided to invade Iraq, Saddam had already been weakened beyond repair. He was indeed nothing but a paper tiger. Everybody knew it. George W. Bush, on the other hand bent over backwards to build the case against Saddam Hussein and to portray him as an imminent danger to world peace. Recall the Axis of Evil. Bush's people even fabricated a connection between Saddam and Al-Qaeda to link him to the events of September 11, 2001. The Neoconservatives in his administration created one lie after another and with the complicity of a national media that seemed at the time incapable of finding the truth or disputing these lies, and these hawks gained the political support to go to war against Iraq. Some argue that the real reason for W's action was the fact that Saddam had planned a failed assassination attempt against Bush senior, who delivered the humiliating defeat to Saddam in Desert Storm years before.

73

So here we were, with our eyes diverted from the real target in Afghanistan. With Bin Laden still at large, we decided to invade a nation that presented no real threat to our national security and had not declared war against us, on the pretext that it might constitute at some future time some sort of danger. Wow, what a way to justify a war! This was an unprecedented rationale never before used in US foreign policy. Well that's what happened, and in the spring of 2003 the U.S. led a massive invasion, and the second war in Iraq was in full swing.

We were going to be greeted as liberators they said, and they claimed it would be a cakewalk. Well, the simple reality is that no country will greet an invading army as liberators. Hence, following the initial success of the military strike, when the U.S. did not withdraw, an unceasing insurgency developed and casualties continue to mount with no end in sight. Claims that the insurgency was in its last throes were made by Cheney many years ago, nonetheless, the realities on the ground tell an entirely different story. So really when will the loss of life finally cease? Easy, when the last American soldier leaves Iraqi soil. This is a no-brainer, and it amazes me that the same conclusion has eluded so many of the so-called "Middle East experts!" The one goal that was achieved by this war was ridding Iraq of Saddam Hussein, but the question remains: was there not another way to accomplish this? Could we not have continued the sanctions and the inspections and tightened the nuts around him to the point where some stronger political figure–aided or unaided—pushed him out of the way? These and similar questions will never be answered, and it may

74

well happen that Iraq may further deteriorate into a fragmented collection of microstates, which is, of course, a recipe for anarchy. W's mantra seems to have been, "don't confuse me with facts—I've already made up my mind!"

Another byproduct of this unfortunate war was the mobilization of Islamic fundamentalist groups which found the Iraqi experience a very convincing argument as to why the US has to be fought throughout the world even with the lives of teenaged kids whose religious zeal is so easy to manipulate in light of our disastrous foreign policy. At this time, the conventional wisdom is that the US has to get out of Iraq ASAP and still find a way to do so while preserving its dignity and the memory of all those lives lost without any good reason and for no meaningful cause. What a dilemma.

Hurricane Egypt

It was just before sunset on a beautiful summer day of 1978 in Alexandria. Dodie and I were enjoying that special Mediterranean breeze while driving on the Cornice in my beloved Fiat 128. Beige in color, with a 1.1 cubic liter engine, this little devil was such a smooth and efficient ride. My Fiat was indeed the little engine that could. This was a far cry from the hand-me-down beaten old thing that my folks had given me a few years earlier. While driving along the Cornice, we had a panoramic view of the beautiful Alexandria skyline on the one side and an unimpeded view of the horizon of the Mediterranean over the waves that were breaking onto the shore. My Fiat took us everywhere that evening, from as far east as the Royal Palace of Montazah, which was in days past the summer residence of the king who had been deposed, and even farther east to Abukir, where we used to enjoy some of the best seafood restaurants in town. This pleasant, uneventful spot on the Alexandria seashore had once witnessed the Battle of the Nile, the naval battle between Napoleon Bonaparte and Admiral Horatio Nelson. But as far as I was concerned, there were bigger fish to fry. As we drove, I remember telling my then fiancé that it might be wise to get out of Egypt soon before the political situation deteriorated any further.

Let me put this into context. The best of times were also the worst of times. Having restored the pride of the Egyptian people along with that of the Arab World, Sadat was considered a war hero for his successful 1973 confrontation with Israel. It would take a couple more years to add to this distinction that of peacemaker. It took his famous six-handed hand shake with Begin and Carter at Camp David for him to earn that title. However, most Egyptians were finding it difficult to make ends meet, but they had been willing to give Sadat a chance to make things better for everybody. It was therefore startling for them to wake up one morning and to learn from the newspapers that—without any warning—the prices of nearly all basic commodities had suddenly skyrocketed. This decision rubbed the people the wrong way. Large demonstrations ensued in the streets of most major cities on the 18th and 19th of January 1977, and the government quickly reversed its actions and things seemed to have gone back to normal. The government promised to ease the hardships of the people, but the public response was a sobering reminder that people can only endure so much. Although Sadat insisted on characterizing those demonstrations as mob riots, they were in reality an authentic expression of his people's frustration and suffering.

To shed some more light on my remark to my fiancé about our departure from Egypt, I would like to draw a comparison to the famous Roadrunner cartoon series. You probably recall the inept villain, Wile E. Coyote. Mr. Coyote would invariably, yet never successfully attempt to set one trap after another for the elusive and incredibly fast protagonist, the Roadrunner. In one such attempt, he carefully positions his ACME cannon on the side of the road and rigs it through an elaborate pulley mechanism so that when the Roadrunner comes into sight he can pull on a rope causing his cannon to discharge its load at his fast moving target. Of course when the moment comes, the mechanism doesn't work as planned, and no matter how hard the Coyote pulls, nothing happens. Frustrated by this turn of events, he climbs onto the cannon and, peering down the barrel, begins to carefully tamp the device. This doesn't work either, so, again to no avail, he starts pounding and banging on it. He finally jumps up and down on the cannon, and when this doesn't produce any effect, he sticks his head in the barrel for a closer look. You know the rest. The cannon discharges leaving him a mess, while the Roadrunner safely passes by with his triumphant "Beep-Beep." What does this have to do with Egypt? Bear with me.

Egypt has a history that reaches back more than 7,000 years, and has experienced more than its share of political unrest, internal turmoil, and foreign occupation. As far back as 1650 BC the Hyksos invaded Egypt and stayed for a good couple of centuries before they were driven out by Ahmose I. In 343 BC it was the Persians' turn, and they invaded and occupied the country for a short time. Later on the Ptolemaists took over Egypt and lasted until their last ruler Cleopatra, who committed suicide after her failed love affairs, first with Julius Cesar and then Marc Anthony. The Romans were in Egypt until the Byzantine era that flourished during the early days of Christianity. It was in AD 639 that Egypt became part of the Islamic Empire. In 1250 the country was ruled by the Mamluks who stayed in power until 1517 when the Ottoman Empire became the new powerhouse in Egypt. A brief occupation by the French took place in the period between 1798 and 1801, and was followed by the Dynasty of Muhammad Ali, which in turn ruled Egypt all the way down to the British Protectorate that lasted from 1882 until the revolution of 1952.

The thing to note about these millennia of ups and downs is that the Egyptians always exhibited an ability to tolerate injustice for prolonged periods of time to the point where everyone, including the invaders, believed that their spirits had been broken and that they would never reassert themselves. Yet even after prolonged periods of submission, the Egyptians would always revolt. Their boiling point is impossible to predict, but watch out, because when they do revolt, they mean business.

Do you recall the Wile E. Coyote cartoon mentioned above? Well let's just say that the Egyptian people are analogous to the ACME cannon which endures beating after beating but finally goes off when least expected.

When I left Egypt in 1979 to pursue my graduate studies in the US, I thought that I had made it out of there just before the explosion. However, I was completely off the mark. The Egyptian cannon remained silent for decades to follow. It was as if I were standing there with my fingers in my ears fearing an explosion that did not finally arrive until thirty odd years later!

On January 25, 2011 masses of Egyptian people demonstrated against the regime. They had one demand: that President Hosni Mubarak step down. Ground zero for the protestors became the main square in downtown Cairo, Al Tahrir Square. Similar gatherings occurred in other major cities and throughout the country, particularly Alexandria and Suez. The precursor to this uprising was a similar event in the North African country of Tunisia a month earlier. That revolution resulted in the deposition of the former president Zine El Abidine Ben Ali. Armed with nothing more than their resolute will and human dignity, the Egyptians utilized modern social networking including Facebook, Twitter, and text messaging, to organize them and come out en masse with unflinching vigor and determination. In this, they resembled the Nile floods whose enormous and unstoppable currents wash forward and push aside whatever stands in their way. I watched CNN's coverage of this historic event in awe. The great nation and ancient civilization was rising once again to stand up to a ruler who had been an utter failure for thirty years and had delivered nothing but misery, oppression, and crippling economic woes. The country had been under emergency law for decades on end, and vice presidency had remained vacant since Mubarak's taking power in 1981 following the assassination of Sadat. This was a deliberate act by a cunning man who was buying time to groom his son to continue the dictatorship subsequent to his retirement. And why not? It appeared to have worked for Hafez Al Assad of Syria who paved the way for his own son to take over at his departure. His son Bashar now faces the unenviable task of putting down a civil uprising not much different from the one that took place in Egypt. He seems to be determined to rule the Syrians even no matter how many of them he has to kill to succeed! But that's another story.

To set the record straight, we are talking about a totalitarian regime that governed Egypt with an iron fist and had no qualms about terrorizing its own civilian population, shamelessly rigging elections, and throwing all who showed interest in the office of the presidency in prison for years on end. One such example was Dr. Ayman Noor who dared to run against Mubarak in the presidential elections of 2005. This was a regime that acted as if it owned the country and its resources and allowed corruption to run rampant leaving no hope for honest, ordinary people for their own future or that of their children.

Watching the demonstrations on TV, I saw one young man explain his position to a reporter. He stated that Americans had voted for five presidents since Mubarak had come to power. All he wanted was a chance to vote in an election that hadn't been rigged. Was that too much to ask? How telling were his comments! We often do not appreciate our blessings until we see others who lack them. One banner in Al Tahrir square read, "Yes, we too can!" How about that?

Let me give you my two cents worth on the politics of the Middle East. Think about the following universal political model (UPM), and let's for the sake of convenience call it the Middle East UPM. This model consists of a head of state (president, king, prince, or what have you), his immediate family, a larger circle of followers (beneficiaries or hangers on are more accurate terms), and, finally, the rest of the nation. In this UPM, the head of state has absolute power, and he and his family are entitled to take whatever they want of the nation's wealth. The beneficiaries, to a lesser degree, can make similar claims to the national resources—only they have to kick back part of their profits to the ruler and, perhaps, his family members. But what is their thought for the population at large? Well, as a modern Mary Antoinette might put it, "Let them eat sand!"

83

Let's proceed from this sketch of a Middle East UPM to the fun part. All you have to do is name a dictator, and your model will adapt itself to his respective country. For Mubarak, the model adapts itself to Egypt, for Assad, to Syria. For Ali Abdullah Saleh, and the model fits Yemen to a tee, and on and on you go. Names of dictators and nations may change, yet the model remains constant. This goes a long way to explaining why there are similar uprisings in many of these states. Just look at their populations as the bottom tiers in the various embodiments of this Middle East UPM, and you'll have a perfect understanding of the current situation in this volatile part of the world.

It took the revolution to deliver Egypt's first democratically elected president ever! This took only a year and a half. Not bad for a 7,000-year-old civilization that had never elected a president before! But let me digress for a moment and tell you about these historic elections and their final outcome. In conformity with the constitutional guidelines, thirteen candidates were qualified to run in those elections. So if you are the superstitious type, that number might already have given you an uneasy feeling. Of those candidates, some were libertarians, some were independents, some belonged to the Muslim Brotherhood's "Party of Liberty and Justice," some were Islamic Fundamentalists representing "The Party of Light"—and believe it or not, some were remnants of the old regime.

In my own mind, I thought that the previous Minister of the Exterior, Mr. Amr Moussa was the best choice. He was the one candidate who had a long political career, and who had publically expressed his disagreement with Mubarak's regime. Because of this position, he had been kicked upstairs to the post of General Secretary of the Arab league, and as a result of his "promotion" he had been removed from the domestic political scene for the ten years leading up to the revolution. He is well-known to the international community, and specifically, to the Arab World, with whose leaders he had very strong ties, and by whom he is highly regarded. This man would have hit the

84

ground running; something that I thought was vital at this critical junction in this nation's history. But what do I know? After the first round of elections, Moussa ended up in a disappointing fifth place.

Since the rule was that a clear winner after the first round needed more than 50% of the vote, we headed into a second between the top two finishers. This was a problem. The top finisher was Dr. Muhammad Morsi of the Muslim Brotherhood who represented their Party of Liberty and Justice, while in a close second was General Ahmad Shafik, the Minister of Aviation in Mubarak's regime. And worse yet, he was Mubarak's final choice for his own replacement as prime minister. General Shafik had only held this latest title for the last two weeks of the regime as Mubarak undertook his last efforts to control the revolution. Mubarak failed at this because his positions were always one step behind what the demonstrators wanted, while the demonstrators, on the other hand, were continually increasing their demands.

The rub is that Dr. Morsi represented the Muslim Brotherhood, a group to whom the people of Egypt had entrusted their first elected parliament, only to be disappointed a few months later by their dismal performance. The Brotherhood had demonstrated in the lower chamber their utter ignorance of politics by focusing their attention on inconsequential and trivial matters, while leaving the major problems of the nation unaddressed. At that point most people were certain that they had made a grave mistake by voting them in. So why then did Morsi place so well in the first round? Well, because of the Muslim Brotherhood's broad base and their excellent mobilization skills. This organization has always been known for their ability to play the elections game, if not to rule. I would opine that if they were to nominate a rock, you could count on it to win!

Now one might ask: what about General Shafik? What was the voters gripe with him? Well, here people had a more serious problem. As noted, this gentleman was the embodiment of the regime against which people had revolted in the first place. Where else but in Egypt might one find the last prime minister of an ousted regime not only compete but come in second in the race for the presidency? Amazing! We headed into the second round to determine the first elected president of Egypt, and the people gave their vote to one candidate not as much because they believed in him and his policies, but rather because they were so set against the other. Does that ring any bells? Well, this was a classic case of cutting one's nose to spite one's face. What a dilemma. As expected, the second round was quite heated and nearly ended in a dead heat with Morsi only managing to win by a very small margin. And now there is a president of the land of the pharaohs.

I cannot resist making a few comparisons between Morsi and myself! Why on earth would I want to do that? Well indulge me for a moment here, and you'll understand. For one thing, both of us graduated college in 1975 with degrees in civil engineering. The only difference is that he graduated from Cairo University while my degree was from Alexandria University. Likewise, we both travelled to the USA for graduate school. He got his doctorate from the University of Southern California while I earned mine at Clemson University. And by the way, we both wear gray beards as part of our observance of the same religion. And there is yet another very important similarity between the two of us. Neither of us is qualified to hold the office of the presidency of Egypt. So what is the problem here? Well, one of us is currently occupying that seat! I will venture to say that we can both perform highly sophisticated structural analyses; something that is fine in its own right, but unfortunately, it qualifies neither of us to lead a nation. The comparison ends here. The real difference is that while we are both devout Muslims, he chose to go at it through the Brotherhood, while I would never belong to any such organization. Note that the Muslim Brotherhood is based on a rigid hierarchal system that requires of its members the utmost loyalty and complete submission to their religious leader, their Murshid, a title which can be translated from Arabic into English as "Religious Guide." Some political experts attribute the quick rise of Morsi within the Brotherhood to the extent of his conformity to the views of the Murshid. Now do not forget that because this group had been banned from Egyptian political life for so many decades, as a matter of survival it had become extremely disciplined and introverted. To function in the face of adversity it demanded from all its members strict adherence to its agenda.

Is there hope, then, in this current set up? The simple answer is that it all depends on whether or not President Morsi will be able to remove himself

87

from under the Brotherhood's umbrella. If he is capable of doing so—something about which I have serious doubts—he stands a chance to succeed. But if he rules a country as profoundly complicated, as Egypt, with the enormous challenges it is facing, he will fail miserably if he does so with the mindset of the Brotherhood. I am not that optimistic, but only time will tell.

88

Alexandria Cornice

http://upload.wikimedia.org/wikipedia/
commons/f/f6/Alexcoast.jpg

The Great Recession

So how did it all get started? Well, the driving force behind the train wreck was the housing market. The first several years of the new millennium saw the rise of real estate prices to levels never before seen. This was the modern day equivalent of the gold rush. Home prices kept escalating at a feverish pace and, along with them, the greed of the entire nation. Many Americans wanted a piece of the action, and banks threw caution to the wind and qualified millions of clients for loans they would not be able to sustain. Realtors pushed credulous buyers into homes that were far beyond their means, appraisers' valuations rose in agreement with the ever-increasing price curve, and last but not least many Americans jumped in hoping for a quick buck. It was a big party, but even the best of parties must end, and in the spring of 2007 the housing market came to a screeching halt. The game could not attract any more players, and everyone stood watching the inevitable collapse of what was supposed to be a sure thing. The nation lost in equity a fortune that it could not afford to lose, and panic ensued. Buyers defaulted on their loans, and a massive wave of foreclosures swept through the land. These loans became toxic and eventually polluted Wall Street where investors were left holding financial products composed of recycled real estate loans that were worth next to nothing. By the fall of 2008, major financial institutions teetered on the brink of collapse, and Wall Street itself seemed about to fall apart, and along with it the entire economy. Millions of Americans lost their jobs, and there seems to be no end in sight for this disaster.

While fixing part of the fence between our two properties, my good friend and neighbor Mark, who is employed in the health industry, told me about his experience with real estate investment. He said that during the boom, he bought a rundown house, renovated it, and flipped it a few months later for a cool profit of over a hundred grand. Back then he believed he was a remodeling genius and bought himself another property in order to repeat the move. Only this time, he didn't do as well. As prices fell, he tried without success to unload the property. Those who managed to hold on to their property were now holding on to upside down mortgages worth more than their property's current value. What a sad testament to our time!

Economics is certainly a funny business, although it is a modern science with mathematical models and well established theories, it is underlain by a reality that theories cannot sufficiently describe or even account for: consumer confidence. When confidence in the economy begins to evaporate, its problems are compounded. Businesses shrink as banks hold on to their money, afraid to lend. Nothing gets done, and a downward spiral ensues. This is reflected in the collective psychology of the nation, and everybody feels bad.

• •

Whenever I am in the mood for a pizza, I head for a small mom and pop restaurant in my neighborhood. This is no big franchise, just a good old pizza parlor owned by some really nice folks who recently came here from Bulgaria. They make, without a doubt, the best pizza in town. As a regular customer, I am well known to Maria, the owner, and we chat while my pizza is in the oven. One day, on my way back from work, I called in my order as usual, and as I entered the store, I noticed that Maria was not in a good mood. Her sad face rested in the palm of her hand, and her mind seemed to be elsewhere. I tried to cheer her up by asking her what was wrong. She replied, "You know, we went through tough times back in Sophia, and when we came to America, we hoped very much for a better life for ourselves and our kids. But look at this mess we're in now." Maria sighed and added, "It seems that no matter where I go, somehow I manage to attract bad luck. I guess it must be me, then."

I reassured Maria that she cannot hold herself responsible for the biggest economic collapse in recent times, and a shadow of a smile appeared on her face.

I had a similar experience with my good buddy Mike. He worked with me at the office, and we had seen some good times together back in the good old days when construction was booming. Like me, Mike is also an immigrant, only he comes from the former Yugoslavia.

When our business was doing particularly well, we solicited the help of Dusan, a young draftsman also from the former Yugoslavia. This junior designer remained with us for a few months before heading back home to finish his studies in architecture. On one occasion he asked me how I felt about living in this country, and I gave him the honest response that I felt grateful to have had the opportunity to live in the United States. This is where my kids' future is. This is home, and I am an American by choice, not by default. When I noticed that Dusan was surprised at this response, and I asked the reason for his question, he told me that he was amazed by the stark difference in the views on this subject given to him by Mike and me. I do understand Mike's sense of desperation, especially after his immersion in the Bosnian War for years before he found a refuge in America.

I realized that for new immigrants who have not yet managed to establish themselves, the recent economic hardships have left deep wounds, and somehow feel these recent economic difficulties more acutely than do others. I think this may be due to the fact that these folks have worked heroically to create new lives for themselves and their families in this country, and they have done so with elevated expectations about the definition of a decent and a good life. Therefore, they are all the more disappointed when their hopes crash after all they suffered before they came here. I can understand how hard this must be for them to swallow.

94

As a young child, when I felt bad, my mother would reassure me that everything would turn out alright. Sometimes I doubted her optimism, but you know what, everything eventually turned out just as she said it would! Today, I have no doubt that everything will be fine with America. Hardships will fade away, the economy will improve, and unemployment will be reduced. Even if it takes longer than we had hoped, we will come back stronger and wiser than we were. I think that my mother's words to me were not just meant to comfort me, but additionally to declare her faith in the strength of her son. It is with similar love and faith in this country that I am telling you that it is going to be alright. Just you wait and see!

Hossam and Mike, Walnut creek CA 2012

(Private collection)

Internal Affairs

Both my sister and I attended private schools, and as early as our preschool years we were equally fluent in both the Arabic and English languages. Although we both were also involved in extracurricular activities such as music and sports, she was not as keen about academics. On my monthly report card, I was invariably on top of my class, while my sister rarely brought home a report card without a few failing grades. Nevertheless, while Dad would closely examine my grades and declare that some of my As were not good enough, he would readily sign off on my sister's report—at times trying very hard not to smile at his daughter's mischief. I must have been in middle school when I overheard a conversation between my parents about our education. Mom was arguing with Dad about his double standard in this matter; she objected to him being hard on me for my straight As while giving my sister's multiple Fs a free pass. He calmly replied that he wanted me to grow up to be a tough young man. Yet this double standard did not at all bother me because I had already figured out that he was secretly pleased with my report card, proud of his only son, and this was his way of encouraging me to do my best. I must point out; however, that Dad's generation was probably the last to apply this double standard. I know that I was gender blind when it came to my own kids' education.

Just as my parents made sure that we ate right and grew up in good health, they also made sure that we grew up with healthy and able minds. They desired that we should be ready to take on the world, and they clearly wanted us to understand the world owed us nothing. If we wanted a place in the sun, we'd better excel in our education. The parents of our friends had the same understanding and paid a great deal of attention to their children's education, as well. My Dad often told me that all worldly possessions could be lost, but not education; knowledge cannot be taken away, and education is the only reliable and true fortune in life.

I still recall how Mom would point to the University of Alexandria's school of engineering as we drove by it, and tell me that this was going to be my school when I was old enough. The school was very impressive with its towering Pharaohic architectural style and was indeed a sight to be admired. Needless to say, I fell in love with the place, and not too long after that I would end up spending five wonderful years there studying to become an engineer.

Comparing the Egyptian educational system to its American counterpart, I have noticed that the former offered a natural transition from high school to college, while in the case of the US, the transition is almost a qualitative leap. In the American case, the abrupt transition results from the laxity of grade school curricula in the face of college-level work which demands a much higher level of commitment. Nowadays, we let our kids get away with murder all the way through high school, and they have no meaningful contact with reality until college, where they face expectations way higher than what they are used to. American universities are among the best there is. The only proof you need is the great numbers of international students trying to get into them. On the other hand, our school system needs a major overhaul to bring it up to the level where it can compete with the rest of the industrial world. You only need to take a look at how our children perform in math, science, reading, and problem solving to realize that we are not even close. The Program for International Student Assessment (PISA) is a survey conducted every three years of the knowledge and skills of 15-year-olds in the major industrialized countries. This collaboration between participating nations is administered by the international nongovernmental organization, the Organization for Economic Cooperation and Development, (OECD), and to develop valid comparisons across countries and cultures it draws on the expertise of the world's leading educators.

Well over a quarter of a million students in 41 countries took part in the most recent two-hour examination which was administered by their own schools. All 30 OECD member countries participated in the 2011 study, as did 11 partner countries.

The sad reality is that the US did not do well compared to the rest of the world. Out of 41 nations, our students ranked 28th in math, 22nd in science, 18th in reading, and 22nd in problem solving. Something has got to change.

When my kids were in high school, the sentiment of their school counselors was that to avoid hurting their self-esteem or something along those lines we shouldn't push them too hard. This approach did not sit well with Dodie and me, as you can see from the following conversation she had during a conference with the academic counselor regarding my son's college applications. My son was present, and for this reason, it reminds me of my parents' conversation about my education I overheard when I was in middle school.

Counselor: You don't have to pressure him into going to college if he doesn't want to go. Let him explore his options and he'll find the way that's right for him.

Dodie: So what are you proposing for him?

Counselor: Why not let him try a couple of years at community college so he can decide what he wants to do?

Dodie: No, no, no, you don't understand! We did not raise our kids to end up in community colleges. For years we've been preparing these kids to compete for spots in the best colleges of California!

Counselor: But you might be applying too much pressure on them.

Dodie: Well, life is tough.

All our kids attended good universities, they all graduated, and they are taking the first steps of their professional careers.

We need immediately to start fixing our K–12 educational system and stop worrying so much about making our kids work hard. I am sure that the late president Reagan—a man who I really liked—was only joking when he declared, "hard work never killed anybody, but… why take the chance!"

Capitalism 2.0

Remember what I mentioned earlier about places being similar to people? So whereas Chicago was an unfortunate experience for me, I have just had the opposite to that with Walnut Creek, California. This small town in the East Bay and I are so at ease with one another that whenever I am not in a good mood, all I have to do is take a stroll downtown for my mood to invariably get better. With its restaurant stretch along Locust Street, I am guaranteed to come across a restaurant to my taste on any given day, and with its outdoors shopping mall — Broadway Plaza — shopping is such an enjoyable affair especially when it is complemented by some beautiful sound tracks that fill the air with the sounds of old blue eyes among many other giants.

On this particular autumn day, I was enjoying the breeze as I headed towards one of the best Italian restaurants in town where I was to meet a few friends for dinner. As we chatted while having our meal, one of those friends — known for his strong republican beliefs — made an argument that the progress of this country was driven by a combination of two driving forces, namely; greed and fear. And even with his eloquent attempts trying to make his point, I could not help but think to myself would it not have been better if such forces were based instead on ambition and compassion? That way the whole premise would be magically transformed from negative to positive driving forces and the whole society would be an integral unit instead of disenfranchised fragments of humans. Anyway, since I was not ready to trade savoring my fettuccini with being dragged into a heated political argument, I kept my mouth busy with the former rather than the latter!

Later that night though, my mind wondered at how fundamentally different were the conceptions of our two main political parties about what was best for the country, and how to go about achieving it. So here you have Capitalism which is based on free enterprise and allowing supply and demand to be the deciding factor when it comes to the exchange of labor and goods, all of which is to be undertaken by the private sector for profit with no intervention from government. As a result of the overemphasis on individual investor's profit, e.g. shareholders, workers and for that matter the society at large take a back seat. If you couple this ideology with an economic crisis that left millions of hardworking, honest, middle class Americans struggling to keep their heads above the water, you may understand what prompted numbers of individuals to flock into what emerged into the "Occupy Movement." The first

104

such movement was the "Occupy Wall Street" which started in New York City's Zuccotti Park on September 17, 2011. These individuals were protesting the disparity in wealth and how this was destabilizing the foundation of democracy. These views were echoed by so many groups all around the world and the movement became universal. So is there any merit to such claims? Well, let's take a look at a couple of the wealthiest people that Capitalism had produced. What did Bill Gates and William Buffet end up doing after acquiring their monumental fortunes?

105

In 1994, the William H. Gates Foundation was formed with an initial stock gift of $94 million. In 1999, the foundation was renamed the Bill & Melinda Gates Foundation. After a merger with the Gates Learning Foundation in 2000, Gates gave an additional $126 million. During the foundation's following years, funding grew to $2 billion. On June 15, 2006, Gates announced his plans to transition out of a day-to-day role with Microsoft, effective July 31, 2008, to allow him to devote more time to working with the foundation.

Buffett is a U.S. businessman and philanthropist. As chairman and chief executive officer of Berkshire Hathaway Inc., he has invested in a broad range of companies, from See's Candies to Geico Insurance to Fruit of the Loom. In 2006, Buffett pledged most of his fortune to the Gates Foundation and to four charitable trusts created by his family—the Susan Thompson Buffett Foundation, the Howard G. Buffett Foundation, the Susan A. Buffett Foundation, and the NoVo Foundation (led by Peter A. Buffett.) His gift to the Gates Foundation of 10 million shares of Berkshire Hathaway stock, to be paid in annual installments, was worth approximately $31 billion in June 2006.

Both these great men joined their forces and adopted a policy of philanthropy wherein they donated large portions of their fortunes to help their fellow man wherever it is needed all over the world with three major programs:

1. Global Health Program

2. Global Development Program

3. United States Program

So do the efforts of Gates and Buffet go against the grain of Capitalism, or do they represent a much needed adjustment to that system to adapt to the realities of a changing world? It seems that Capitalism needs to be tweaked to account for a more humane treatment of the majority instead of just focusing on the interests of the wealthy minority.

The truth is that Americans have no problem with anybody acquiring wealth; as a matter of fact they look up in admiration to those who are successful as they strive to accomplish similar feats for themselves and their loved ones in this wonderful land of opportunities. However, they become uneasy when the economic gap widens to unprecedented measures and it becomes harder and harder to hold on to the American Dream.

In an attempt to find a fair measure of the economic gap, let us consider the average estimated top-to-bottom pay ratio in a large number of companies operating in the USA. Online salary database PayScale.com ran the numbers on median pay of all workers at each company in the Fortune 50 list then compared that pay number to the annual CEO pay at each company. While Warren Buffet takes home a humble 10 times what his average employee earns, other CEOs' incomes are hundreds or thousands of times higher than the typical worker they employ. In the UK, the ratio is about 15:1 in the public sector and about 262:1 in the private sector. Some economists claim that a ratio of around 20:1 is a good rule of thumb, so how can we reconcile this with a company such as UnitedHealth Group wherein the ratio is 1737:1? The only word that comes to mind in that regards is obscene!

Capitalism needs a face lift, and it needs it bad. So what do you think will happen if greed prevented the wealthy from making the necessary adjustments? Well, the gap will widen even further and there will come a point when groups such as the Occupy Movement will take sharper forms and gain more traction all around the world. This will be the real threat to socioeconomic stability and who knows where this will lead us to.

Now What?

In the fall of 2008, when the presidential campaigns were in their final sprint up to the November elections, the US economy was on the brink of collapse. The practices of Wall Street, the banking system, and the housing market compounded the problem of the massive deficit that came with the squandering of thousands of lives and billions of dollars in the Arabian Desert over the preceding five years. This was a perfect storm, an economic crisis paralleled in our nation's history only by the Great Depression. What a nightmare it was. At that point the 2008 race had narrowed to McCain and Obama. After the national conventions of both parties, only a month before the economic crisis, polls indicated a tight race for the White House, and if I were a betting man, my money would have been on McCain. Why, you ask? Well, I did not believe that Americans would actually put an African American in the White House. It was as blunt as that. I dare venture that, had it not been for the economic collapse, we might have ended up with a Republican president! You see, up to late summer 2008, McCain made no bones about his own lack of knowledge of economic matters and even bragged about it. His position was that the economy would somehow work itself out. He claimed that the only really important issue was national security, and his personal version of the Beach Boys classic, "bomb… bomb… bomb, bomb Iran," is all that many people outside the US now recollect about his understanding of the subject. Such were his thoughts about national security and foreign policy, and so much for his contribution to America's image throughout the world! Obama, on the other hand, kept his focus on both matters, and so when you know what hit the fan, voters were left with the choice between a candidate with a detailed economic plan wrapped up and ready for delivery and someone who had proudly affirmed his own ignorance on the subject. McCain's personal interpretation of *Laissez Faire* came back to bite him when the outcome of the race came to be regarded by many voters as a matter of life and death. Under the rules of this new game, jokes about the economy had become political suicide. You know the rest of the story.

The anti-Obama sentiment became more evident after he became the first black man in the history of this great nation to win the presidency. Childish fits of rejection manifested themselves in reactions such as the "Birther" movement, which seeking to challenge the legitimacy of Obama's presidency makes the erroneous and unfounded claim that he was not born on American soil. Many others, including prominent pundits and politicians, have maliciously subjected the president to ludicrous and humiliating Nazi comparisons. Still others have even gone so far as to incite the public to harm the president—at times both directly and indirectly attempting to stir up racist sentiments through references to lynching.

At the time of this writing, a very heated debate is under way on health care reform, a debate that is long overdue. As ordinary Americans suffer from the ruthless grip of the predatory and manipulative insurance industry, other Western nations are watching in amazement as this debate unfolds. They cannot comprehend why the US, the richest nation on earth, does not have a plan that covers everybody. Most of them have come to the conclusion that universal coverage is the only dignified way for an affluent nation to treat its own people, especially given the fact that there are so many successful models out there to study and adapt to a model that would better serve the American people.

What do we need to do now? Well, after eight years we finally have another intelligent president in the White House, and he is working tirelessly to rescue what can only be described as a sinking ship. He has managed to plug many of the leaks, but full recovery is still a way off. On the national level, it has become evident that our previous toleration for corporate greed and unchecked financial systems cannot provide answers to our nation's economic troubles, and there seems to be no way to maintain economic and social stability without some form of government oversight. Some people still claim that government is the problem, and some of them cry socialism. Well, let them cry!

On the international front, however, we need to capitalize on the great admiration that our president has earned and rebuild the bridges that were broken by the idiocy and narrow mindedness of past administrations. Let's treat others as what they are, as human beings with whom we share the planet. You can't expect much cooperation from them if you treat them like a group of immature children who need us to tell them what to do. A dignified president such as Obama is in a much better position to succeed at treating others with the respect and dignity they deserve and expect. When you show your good side, people reciprocate. You are much more likely to gain people's hearts and minds when you are not at the same time making land grab. Provide economic support and help the moderate elements flourish, and you will establish a new generation of America lovers instead of haters. Along with other measures, this approach will weaken the bases of fundamentalism all over the world. And finally, when push comes to shove, for goodness sake, do not send our army anywhere but on missions which are absolutely necessary, which are fully and properly defined, and which suit their training and their capacity. The armed forces are not equipped to police a civilian population, or to babysit somebody else's civil war, nor are they equipped to fight guerilla warfare. Examples from our nation's recent history of conflicts meeting the above criteria include WWII and, closer to the present time, the first gulf war. Imagine that! Indeed, none of our other military encounters were necessary. What a waste of life and resources. And when the need arises, there are always covert operations to tackle problems such

112

as terrorism. These missions can be carried out efficiently and in secrecy with much less damage abroad and at home. Furthermore, why don't we shift our policy toward greater utilization of unmanned interventions such as those carried out by Drones and similar technology? Wouldn't that be a wiser choice? Let us advance our technology and give our men and women in the military a better chance to live full, long, productive, and healthy lives instead of destining them to suffer horrendous injuries in unnecessary wars. Is this so hard to do?

113

In short, why not change the unfavorable image created by some of our previous leaders? Let's replace it with the vision of the humane, caring, and peaceful people that we really are. Let the beacon of freedom and liberty shine forth and spread its guiding light all over the world. Let it shine over the entire world so that... well I have to say it: "Yes We Can!!"

We are now fast approaching the 2012 November presidential elections, and barring any unforeseen circumstances, it looks like it is going to be a race between President Obama and Mitt Romney. So let's review what Obama accomplished during his first term. For starters, he inherited the mega-mess left to him by his predecessor. He was handed a patient bleeding to death from unneeded surgery, whose condition he finally managed to stabilize. Does that mean that the patient is fully recovered? Of course not. America has a long recovery period before her, and she requires proper nourishment until she can manage for herself. Everybody knows that this kind of transformation does not happen overnight. And, if you are the patient type, you already know as much. But our current economic condition is what it is, and there is no magic wand or any easy fix. Sometimes we just have got to roll with the punches.

Another thing this good man had done has been to reverse the unprecedented rate of job loss, and we are beginning to see positive results. Unemployment rates have dipped from around 12% to about 8%. Is this a great accomplishment? Absolutely! Could it have been brought about a little faster? Absolutely! And how would the president have done that? He could have been tougher about getting his way in Washington. He paid way too much attention to the obstructionist moves by his Republican opposition. This tougher approach will be necessary for the implementation of his policies when he is reelected to his second term. Note that I didn't say "if" reelected; I said, "when." So do I walk around with a crystal ball? Not really, but I am putting it on paper, Obama is going to win! What else has he accomplished? How about his health care plan? Because it is such an unpopular measure, short-sighted politicians will invariably ignore the benefit it represents; nonetheless, it is probably the single most effective political decision with strong repercussions for our economy for generations to come. Again, this is something that does not necessarily appeal to folks, both politicians and citizens, interested in looking out for themselves and no one else. And by the way, the Supreme Court had just upheld a ruling in favor of the president's plan. Did Obama do anything else worth mentioning? Oh yeah, HE KILLED Bin Laden!!

114

So now, who do you want to put in the White House? A guy who had done all the above, still manages to remain connected to the common man, and nevertheless has time to shoot some hoops with his buddies? Or would you prefer Mitt Romney, a guy so out of touch with that same common man that he can only gesture in amazement at doughnuts in a neighborhood deli and only manage to identify them as "those chocolate goodies?!" This, of course, is from the representative of a political party that will not cease in its attempts to portray the president as an elitist. You can be certain that Mitt knows what a croissant is. As you might expect, this performance had absolutely no chance of escaping David Letterman's Top 10 List. According to Dave, these are some Mitt's other ways of referring to doughnuts:

10. Powdered snack cylinders
9. Dessert Bagels
8. Leavened Batter Globules
7. Sugary Pastry Tires
6. Perforated Strudel Orbs
5. Saturated Fat Wheels
4. Dunking Muffins
3. Glazed Giddy-Ups
2. Chris Christie Kremes
1. The Cadillac of Pastries

So, how is Obama to prepare for the upcoming debates? Well, all he has to do is to just wait for Romney to finish and say, "Yeah, but you didn't kill Bin Laden!"

115

In all seriousness, when it comes to his record, the president has nothing to be ashamed of. All he has to do next is be more forceful in pushing forward his agenda because tough times call for tough measures. Had he adopted this policy early on in his first term, he would have accomplished more than he actually did. Give the guy a chance to finish what he started.

I know that the president's campaign staff is struggling to come up with a slogan as powerful as the one they used last time around, and their problem is understandable given that the previous one is so hard to match. So why not just bring the winner up-to-date? How about, "Yes we can—just let us finish!"

117

President Barack Obama

http://leighb.com/election08.htm

Epilogue

My Dad: For the most part, Dad enjoyed very good health. He used to claim that the only reason he ever went to the dentist was to drive one of us there. Indeed, he had immaculate white teeth and was very particular about health matters in general. His weakness, however, was his respiratory system, and he suffered increasingly from asthma in the latter part of his life. He suspected that this condition was the result of his exposure to chemicals during his lab work. I think he may have been right about that, because of that smell of chemical fumes on his clothing at the end of my school days when I would ride home with him. My middle school was next door to his lab. As anyone with asthma will tell you, Asthma attacks are often instigated by chemicals and by natural irritants including pollen dust, or by high humidity which encourages the growth of mold. Since we lived in Alexandria right on the Mediterranean Sea, there was no escaping this, either. The attacks would leave him exasperated and drained. It was no surprise;

therefore, that he would be extremely careful to avoid catching colds, which would invariably turn into those dreaded bouts. When he was the dean, he would not allow any paper work into his office that arrived from the office of anybody he knew to be suffering from a cold or the flu. He understood only too well how much he would suffer if he were to get sick, and he took every precaution to safeguard his health.

Dad paid close attention to my applications for graduate study in the US. He wanted me to have the same opportunity he had had years before, and he was even more enthusiastic about the matter than I was, especially after my test scores came back indicating that my chances of acceptance were quite good.

In the last few years of his life, he and I became a lot closer than we were when I was a child. When I was growing up he was quite tough with me regarding my education, but later on he began to relax because I was progressing well. We used to shoot pool and chat about life, and I think he enjoyed those encounters as much as I did.

His final asthma attack hit him especially hard, so I drove him to the hospital in my little Fiat. His heart could no longer take the strain, and he died there on April 12th, 1979. He was fifty nine. His death was devastating for me and the rest of the family, and there was no consolation for me when I returned that same day from the hospital to find my letter of acceptance to the University of Notre Dame. Dad never got a chance to celebrate with me.

It has been more than thirty years since Dad left us, and I wish he were still around as part of my life and more importantly, my kids' lives. They would have benefitted from his kindness as much as I did.

My Mom: As with all moms, she provided the much-needed TLC to my sister and me. She was passionate and very protective of her offspring. She always made sure we ate right, dressed right, and behaved properly. The atmosphere in our household was happy and enjoyable. The peace was at times disrupted by arguments with Dad, which would occasionally escalate into a train ride to Cairo, where she would spend a few days with her parents. After things cooled down, she would come back, and we would be at the station anxiously awaiting her arrival.

Mom visited us twice in the US; she came to South Bend in 1981 and to Clemson in 1983. She tremendously enjoyed herself and, to my great surprise, she developed a passion for the American way of life including food, clothing, and, to my even greater amazement, she fell in love with the music of Stevie Wonder, one of my all-time favorite artists.

After working in Chicago for a couple of years, we lived in Egypt for more than a dozen years before our return to California. During this time, Mom had a chance to see all my kids in their early years. She had reserved Saturday as her day, and we'd go to her place for a nice dinner. This tradition lasted until she fell ill in early 1993 with pancreatic cancer. My mother was a woman of great beauty, but over the following months, we watched her dwindle to a fragile skeleton of skin and bones. She died on November 30th 1993. At the time, my youngest was five, and my eldest, ten.

Dodie: More than 30 years after our marriage, she remains my wife, the love of my life, and the mother of my four kids, and I love all five of them more than anything in the world. She worked in retail for a number of years before returning to her original passion, marketing and advertising. Currently, Dodie is fighting fiercely against breast cancer. She has undergone a lumpectomy and has started her chemotherapy protocol. I know she will pull through, but months of grueling treatment are still ahead. Please remember her in your prayers.

My cousin Dalal: She and her husband returned to Egypt following the 1967 war with Israel, and they have been living in Cairo ever since. They visit us in California every now and then, and she is still my favorite cousin!

King Farouk: After he was deposed on July 23rd, 1952, Farouk never again set foot on Egyptian soil. His yacht carried him to Italy, where he spent the remaining years of his life. He died following what was described as a very heavy meal in an Italian restaurant. Some believe that he was actually poisoned by the revolutionary regime.

Gamal Abdel Nasser: He saw his dream of a unified Arab Nation evaporate following his crushing defeat by the Israelis on June 5th, 1967. He lived a broken man until his death on September 28th, 1970, of a massive heart attack. Many Arab nationalists still consider him the role model for Arab leadership.

Abdel Hakim Amer: In August 1967, General Amer was arrested along with fifty military officers and was accused of conspiring against Nasser. He was put under house arrest, and on September 14th, 1967 he was declared dead from cyanide poisoning in an apparent suicide. Some accounts of this event maintain that he had been given that choice as the alternative to a military trial which would have inevitably led to conviction and a death sentence. Like General Rommel who failed in his conspiracy against Hitler, he took the pill.

Zaki Shashoua: All attempts to reconnect with my good friend Zaki have not yet succeeded. I will keep trying.

Anwar Sadat: As a pragmatic politician, Sadat understood that the best he could do was to achieve peace with Israel. He worked diligently towards this goal, and with the help of President Carter, signed the peace treaty with the Israeli Prime Minister, Menachem Begin. Many in the Arab world considered Sadat to have sold out, and he was seen as a traitor. Radical Islamists infiltrated the troops marching in the October 6th, 1981 military parade, and he was ambushed as he stood to salute them. He died on the spot. Standing next to him, his Vice President, Hosni Mubarak, remained unscathed and became the next Egyptian president.

Ayatollah Khomeini: The supreme leader of the Iranian revolution was very popular among his people. He was held in high esteem and remained in power until his death in 1989 at the age of 86. His anti-

Western stances appealed to Iranian fundamentalists, and he supported the takeover of the American embassy which led to the Iranian hostage crisis. He was of the Shia faith.

Kathleen Fisher: Kathleen and John Fisher and their kids were our host family when we arrived in South Bend, and they have remained part of our lives throughout the years. Kathleen and John are no longer together, and she has since remarried. Their lovely children grew up and scattered across the country and even into Mexico. She and her husband, Bill, came to visit us in 2007. We had not seen her for nearly thirty years, and we had a wonderful time together. She is now retired from her nursing career.

Katie Fisher: No longer the adorable five-year-old, Katie is now a beautiful and equally adorable young woman residing in South Bend where she works as a Yoga instructor. She may still remember you know who!

Nelson Bauld, Jr.: Retired in 1989 from his illustrious career teaching and conducting research. He is currently an emeritus professor at Clemson University.

Rick, Randy and George: Rick and Randy both held teaching positions in South Dakota, where they currently live. Little George has grown up and is now a proud member of the US Air force. By the way, he has a sister I have not yet met. May be someday I will have a chance to visit the Dakotas. Who knows!

Saddam Hussein: Was Vice President to Ahmad Hassan Al-Bakr, from whom he took control of Iraq in a bloodless coup in 1969. He remained president until

2003, when he was ousted by the coalition forces led by America and Britain. He was captured and stood trial for the crimes committed against his people. He was convicted in 2006, sentenced to die by hanging, and on December 30th 2006 he was executed. Prior to his capture, his two sons were killed while resisting arrest by the Americans.

Osama Bin Laden: On May 2, 2011, Operation Neptune Spear was executed by order of President Obama. This move had been planned to perfection by the CIA and carried out by Navy Seals, who raided Bin Laden's residential compound in Abbottabad, Pakistan. They killed Bin Laden, flew his body to Afghanistan for positive identification, and within a day they buried him at sea.

Dusan: Has completed his degree in architecture from the school of architecture in Belgrade. He visited the Bay Area a couple of times and is looking forward to come over and start his career in America.

Mike: When business took a nose dive, Mike decided to seek employment elsewhere. He left my office for over a year before returning to rejoin efforts. Somehow, it seems that we are just destined to work together no matter how good or bad business is. He does some side jobs to supplement his income. He is in a slightly better mood but not quite the optimist yet.

Maria: Traveled to Bulgaria to tend to her ailing mother where she spent a few months. She is back in business and is no longer blaming her fortunes for the bad times. She still makes the best pizza in town.

Hosni Mubarak: After being ousted on February 11, 2011 Mubarak stood trial for his role in not preventing the murder of innocent civilians protesting in the streets of Egypt. He was found guilty and was sentenced to life in prison. He is currently serving the sentence in Torrah prison located near Helwan; a southern suburb of Cairo. He is reported to being in a state of depression and word has it he is suffering from a terminal illness and does not have much time left. Egypt has moved on and his name hardly appears in the media anymore; a stark contrast to the days when his photo would constantly decorate official newspapers day in and day out.

Bashar Al- Assad: Clinging to power with all his military might, Bashar is committed to latching onto the presidency no matter what. Tens of thousands of men, women, and children have died since the uprising in Syria with no end in sight. At the time being, the international community is reluctant to undertake direct measures against the Syrian regime due to the support it is getting from Russia, China, and Iran. International efforts are limited to denouncing the genocide taking place in Syria which is not enough to induce change in the current situation. Factions of the armed forces had broken ranks and joined what is known as the "Syrian Liberation Army." Furthermore, the defection of the Syrian Prime Minister to neighboring Jordan signifies yet further isolation of the Syrian regime. Nonetheless, radical change in the status quo can only be expected if direct international intervention takes place. Until this happens, hundreds of casualties will continue to fall on a daily basis.

About the Author

The author is a licensed professional engineer in the state of California running his own private practice, and teaches part time at Saint Mary's College of California. He holds a Ph.D. in structural engineering.

In addition, he is a published author of a collection of short stories written in the Arabic language. He is a member of the Egyptian Writers Guild. Numerous of his stories have been published in "Al-Ahram;" the major daily newspaper in Egypt, as well as in "October Magazine," a renowned weekly magazine. The author has many technical publications in the field of structural engineering. This is his debut as a writer of a political memoir.

The author was born and raised in Alexandria, Egypt, where he obtained his degree in Civil Engineering from the University of Alexandria, then lived in the United States where he obtained his Master's degree from the University of Notre Dame, and his doctoral degree from Clemson University. He currently resides in Northern California with his wife and four children.

As a citizen of the world, the author comes well equipped to write his views of both worlds, and in the process sheds valuable light upon areas that need a better understanding of the other. In essence, this is an attempt to bring closer the minds and hearts of people from near and far away lands.